THE BLUEPRINT

*The 90-Day Breakthrough to Shift
Your Mindset & Transform Your Life*

Elle Ross

The information in this book represents the perspective of the author as of publication date. It is intended to be educational and not for diagnosis, prescription, or treatment of any health disorders, nor a substitute for financial planning. This book is presented only for informational purposes and may not be suitable for your health needs or goals. This information is not intended to replace the advice or attention of health care professionals. Please make sure to consult with a professional healthcare physician or financial consultant before engaging in some of the activities. The author is in no way liable for any misuse of the material. While every attempt has been made to confirm the information in this book, neither the author nor any affiliates assume any responsibility for inaccuracies, omissions or errors.

For more information, be sure to visit TheElleRoss.com

Cover Design: DesignerXD
Cover Photographer: CW Jacobs
Editing: Heather DeBlieck
Book Layout ©2017 Dream Press Publishing

The Blueprint. Elle Ross —1st ed.

ISBN-13: 978-1544785936
ISBN-10: 1544785933

Printed in the United States of America

Contents

DEDICATION

This book is dedicated to you. You may have felt lost and are seeking guidance to stop poor choices and habits and redirect your energy to create better ones. Begin building the foundation to improve your health holistically. Unveil your true purpose and bring it to the light to shine outward toward others and transform your life from the inside out. Thank you for deciding to take this journey for yourself and overall wellbeing. Acknowledgement is the first step.

ACKNOWLEDGMENTS

When it comes to gratitude and whom I am most thankful for in my life's journey of how I have arrived where I am today, the first people who come to mind are my parents, Gum-Lai and Garrison. They are truly amazing individuals who have taught and instilled so much wisdom within me from a young girl. Even during the occurrences I may have ventured off away from my destined path, they were always there to support me and guide me back to the light. My Mother is the spiritual leader and always encouraged me to keep my head up, stay humble, remain positive and constantly reminds me to maintain the attitude of gratitude; be present in the moment and live in the now. She would always tell me, "Yesterday is a cashed check, tomorrow is a promissory note, today is a gift and all we have." Those little daily reminders have helped keep my mind grounded as well as bring me through challenging times. My Father is the entrepreneur and businessman, and taught me to fail forward toward my dreams. He was always testing out new inventions and ideas, and would never give up. Anytime he failed or had a set back he persevered and would try a different way to bring his idea into fruition. He showed me how to be wise with my money and not spend frivolously. He taught me the importance of building my portfolio, saving money and investing. He was always supportive in anything I wanted to pursue and made sure to attend any event I had whether in sports or on stage. I can call either one at anytime and they will be there to lend an ear and just listen. Thank you, Mom and Dad, I love and appreciate you both more than words can express.

My five siblings, Garisha, Garrison, Deatri, Azias and Azariah. Each of you has contributed in your own unique way. Garisha, thank you for always being available when I needed big sister advice and lending a safe place when I needed it most. Garrison, thank you for teaching me it is okay to take big risks and to think outside the box. Deatri, thank you for always pushing me to be better; you always told me the things I did not want to hear, but most certainly needed to hear, even if it hurt in the moment. Azias, thank you for being my shining light; I like to refer to you as my little big brother because I look up to you so much. You have taught me strength, courage and the power of the mind; you introduced me to the importance of mediation and becoming one with my higher self. Azariah, thank you for your constant contagious energy and zeal for life; your presence alone brings so much love; your peaceful spirit and words of wisdom inspire me every time we speak; you have taught me that even in the darkest hours I am not alone and it always gets better.

My Mr. Wonderful, my boyfriend Eboni, you are my rock; my everything. You have played such a huge role in where I am in my life today. You are my biggest fan, number one supporter, and motivator and encouraged me to write this book. You have watched me grow and are constantly challenging me to be better each day. You have taught me to be patient. You taught me that daily progression is better than none and to stay focused on one goal at a time. I love you beyond the stars and our bond grows deeper each day. You are my best friend and strongest ally. I appreciate you more than you know.

There are so many other people who have impacted my life and have been positive role models along the way. To my closest friends and distant family, I am truly thankful for every one of you.

ABOUT ELLE ROSS

Elle is an ambitious goal getter and risk taker. When she has her mind set on a goal or vision, she works relentlessly toward it each day. It is her dream to help empower and motivate others to make improvements from within. To inspire others to live and lead healthier, holistic lives from the inside outward. Her mission is to teach others to begin to focus inward within themselves, get in tune with their deeper subconscious, and gain greater clarity and self-love through the daily practice of creating self-transformational habits. She is a Holistic Fitness Coach, an author, mentor, entrepreneur, certified personal trainer and offers nutrition planning. Her motto is fitness is more than just the body; it first, most importantly, begins in the mind. Similar to exercising and building our body's muscles, we also must exercise and strengthen the mind. Everything we do in life first stems from the idea and thought, and then we must take consistent action to bring that dream into fruition. She believes that we all have the capability to reach our full potential, as long as we strongly believe in ourselves.

Elle did not start off where she is today, and like many, was once lost. Her path to her BEST SELF began in February 2016. Prior to this month, she was not making the smartest life choices. She was not fully loving and valuing herself holistically. She was in an unhealthy relationship, drinking heavily, eating unhealthy-toxic food, not exercising, and essentially depressed. She went to the doctor to have a health check, and was informed her that her blood sugar levels were high and she was on there verge of becoming diabetic. She was informed that excessive drinking could lead to higher levels and diabetes. She realized immediately that she had been lying to herself and needed to make a lifestyle change if she wanted to get healthier--mind, body and spirit. She then made a commitment to herself to take action. She committed to a 90-day self cleanse of no alcohol, exercising 6 days a week, daily meditation, meal prep, healthy eating, no television, no social media, reading more positive books, getting out of her relationship, practicing gratitude and positivity, and working on personal goals she had been putting off. She created a systematic structure within her life. It was challenging in the beginning, but she stuck to it and stayed consistent. Those daily practices and the routine that she created became imbedded within her. Since, she has maintained those same practices. The 90-days turned into a lifestyle. She is now the healthiest she has ever been and continues to practice those new daily rituals. Her life has changed completely for the better, all through making the choice to become a better version of herself. Taking action, staying consistent, and being fully committed to growing into her full potential! Her Best Self! Now all she wants to do is share her journey and experience with you, in hope that you can accomplish and achieve similar enlightenment, fulfillment and develop into the Best Version of You.

After your journey please make sure to reach out and connect! Community is key to spreading the light that will soon shine around the globe!

Facebook: ElleRoss.Fit | BFITwithElle

Snapchat: @TheElleRoss

Twitter: @TheElleRoss

Google+:   Elle Ross

Instagram: @TheElleRoss

Email: TheElleRoss@gmail.com

Requirements for the Program

> Positive mindset

> Go-getter and ready-to-roll attitude

> Determination

> Willingness to do

> Journal and a good pen or pencil (available for purchase)

> Calendar (link provided to download)

> White art board (**Optional)

> Sticky notes or dry erase marker

> 10-12 pack of durable Tupperware

> Food Scale (**Optional)

"We are what we repeatedly do. Excellence, therefore, is not an act, but a habit" ~Will Durant

"The Journey you choose to make and walk is not dependent on others. It is only dependent on you and your will and desire to succeed. At the end of the day, no one will be there to push you. Your most vital and influential coach and teacher is yourself. SELF ·motivation; SELF sacrifice; SELF determination, drive and consistent effort through strategic action on how to properly navigate to get to your end goal--all while staying true to your core values, morals and beliefs. Not allowing outside distraction to interfere with the journey and process. I am proud of your relentless commitment to SELF!

SELF EMPOWERED LIMITLESS FOCUS!"

Dedicated to Your Success.

In Love and Health,

Elle Ross

Prologue

When we think about health, most think about exercise and what we eat. But it is more than just physical activity and a healthy diet. We must begin from the mind and connect it to the visual aspect of the brain, which is the moral fiber of the body. There are five different dimen-sions. To demonstrate take one of your hands and open it wide, spreading out all your fingers. As I go through the list that follows, begin to bring one finger in at a time to your palm. The five dimensions are 1. Character 2. Morals 3. Mind 4. Body 5. Spirit. You have just created a fist and when all those dimensions are combined and in line working together, you can create a mighty blow. That blow is you holistically becoming something greater than one-dimensional. Anybody can go into the gym and get fit, but when you go and talk to that person, are they men-tally fit? No, most of the time they are about as fit as a newborn baby. But, just as babies learn and grow to evolve into someone greater, we as adults can do the same. Through exercising and refocusing our energy on growth activities, instead of activities that hinder or hold us back, we can achieve our true destiny and full potential.

Many of us get rid of our morals simply because we try to fit into the standard which society has created for us. So your morals become diluted because you are trying to fit into a society that consistently destroys morals. This, consequently, infringes upon your character. Morals and character go hand-in-hand. With bad morals, comes bad character. If you have bad character no one wants to be around you. The only people that want to be around you are those who are just as miserable as you are. Remember, misery loves company. When you begin working toward holistic health and start exercising your mind, you simultaneously exercise your spirit. Whatever your religion or faith is, embrace it because I know there is something good within it. I know it teaches you to become a better person within. Encourage that, because those elements are intertwined and this will influence you to go into the gym because you want a healthy body. Not to fit into societal norms, but because you want to live a long and healthy life. You will have the desire to change and begin to think clearer, speak clearer, and gain greater clarity.

When I rise in the morning there is purpose in every step I take. There is purpose for every thought that comes into my head and there is a defense mechanism for the toxic people that try to enter my life. Because one, my character is strengthened, and two, my morals are in place and set in stone so that no one can break them. Why? Because I began exercising this throughout the course of my new life journey to make sure that I am defending myself against the toxic norm that has been created through society today. This hinders you from being successful because you are pulled in so many different directions. What allows you to become distracted is not having the mental toughness and fitness necessary to identify reality against the illusions. Many of us are not exercising the fitness of the mind. Therefore, we do not have the strength to withstand those subtle traps that are out there to take us off course. Hence, we get sucked into this lifestyle and then learn to make excuses for our behavior ("Awe, it is okay." "Oh, I will start Monday." "Hmm, well I will just have one."), when it goes totally against what you are trying to do and against who you want to become. For example: I am not saying it is bad to have one glass of wine. But I am telling you if you choose to have one glass of wine, you must be strong and definitive to only have that one glass and move on. Most people will have one and then, lacking the mental fortitude to stop at one, will have a second drink, which then turns into three. And before you know it you are drunk, drinking all over again and back to square one. Back into the same poor habits you wanted to escape from. You want to create a **HEALTHY** person in every sense of the word. In developing who you are, you must incorporate that into your **DAILY** activities.

Take a moment to think about your current circumstances. For you to pick up this book there must have been a breaking point. What was your breaking point? There was a pivotal moment when I realized I needed to wake up; which I will disclose in further detail later in the book. In short, there was shocking news given to me from my doctor. She informed me that my blood sugar was getting close to the *Diabetes* mark. WHAT!?!? I thought to myself, I exercise often and eat healthy most of the time. She asked if I drank, I told her not often. I lied and did not disclose how much alcohol I really consumed on a weekly basis. But I was not only lying to the doctor, I was lying to myself. What people fail to realize is that before you open your mouth to lie to someone else, **you are lying to yourself first**. And you are the worst person you can lie to, because you are the first person that is going to experience the most pain from that lie. The person who will sacrifice the most is **you**. All from that one lie. Therefore, you must take time to reflect and truly look at yourself in the mirror and analyze where you are and where you want to be. I will start by disclosing my journey of coming to the light.

My Story

My journey began long before I even thought of writing a book. It started with me looking in the mirror one day and recognizing where I was in comparison to where I wanted to be. I was in a dark place, lost mentally and physically. Originally from Tacoma, Washington, which is 30 minutes south of Seattle. I had decided to pursue my influenced dream of becoming a model and actress. So, I decided to quit my job and move across country to Atlanta, Georgia to live with my aunt. She recommended it would be a better market for a woman of color versus Los Angeles, California; the media and entertainment scene has grown substantially over the years. I decided to take a leap of faith packed what would fit in my car and drove into the unknown. I had the plan in place to prepare and move there, but no direction and vision for when I arrived. That was where I made my first mistake.

Upon arrival, I became lost mentally in the toxicity of what I thought I needed to be, based off societal standards feeding me trash on TV, the radio, the news and especially social media. I would spend time aimlessly scrolling and comparing myself to others. Before I created a social media account I felt free to be me. It was not until I was influenced by friends at the time: "What? You do not have social media? You are missing out! How are you going to stay up to date on what is going on in the world? The latest fashion, music, how to dress, and the current events?" I did not want to miss out. I wanted to fit in and "be in the know."

Before Atlanta and delving into the entertainment world I did not have any social media, and once I created my accounts, it become an instant obsession. Constantly browsing and comparing myself to other models or actors, thinking I was not thin enough, not good enough, not beautiful enough, just not enough. These false illusions of self that I began to form in my mind created eating disorders, body image insecurities, and led me to take drastic measures to be thin in the waist and curvier below. It was all about the *derriere*, which I did not have, but was not willing to get the surgery or injections. As I began to network and meet other models and actors in the community, I began to learn that the people you meet on social media are not what they appear to be. Pictures are powerful and can display anything you want, but it is when you meet the picture in person where you can really decipher whether a person is genuine. Sadly, after I created a social media account, specifically Instagram, I found myself adjusting myself, going against my morals and standards to keep up with what I observed other models and actresses doing to gain popularity. The majority are always at events; the parties, the drinking, the promotions, the selling of seduction and soft porn on your page to get likes and gain followers. I met people with 100k + followers who, in person, have nothing. Some sleeping on a mattress, no car, no solid job, but you would think by their status on social media that they have it all together. They are struggling too, so do not be fooled. Why as a society do we feel this need for acceptance and validation from others? Why do we care what the Kardashians are doing, wearing, eating, and where they are going? When as a society did we lose our sense of self? Self worth? Self-validation? Reality TV has created a facade that people admire. Illusions lead to confusion. And as a people we find ourselves unhappy, overweight, and aimlessly going through the motions. That was me at one point. Trying to be like everyone else and forgetting who I was, going out and drinking way too much. Listening to music and wanting to be single and date here or there, just have fun and live it up. No commitment. Just games. No substance. You only live once, right?

Music is such a huge influence and impact on today's youth and people. When you really listen, and dissect some of the lyrics it is appalling to think these songs are on the top of the charts. Mostly garbage, but you are out there in the club or wherever toasting it up and singing along; pouring another drink at the same time. But what are you really celebrating? Is this living it up? Those are the questions I began to ask myself and they are the questions you must ask yourself.

I would wake whenever I woke, possibly push the snooze button and go through the day unplanned, unorganized and look forward to the weekend or just to the evening. There was always some event taking place or somewhere to go and have a drink with someone. Not just one, but a couple. Wake and do it again the next day. On the weekends, it was even worse because I could drink as much as I wanted and have the whole next day to recover and sleep in. Basically, let the day go to waste. Clothes got more revealing and modeling photos got more provocative. Where was I headed? It was nowhere good and nowhere toward growth. I was digressing. I began to think about the kind of legacy I was leaving behind. The story I was portraying and selling to young women. I want to be treated as a *Queen*, as a respectable woman; but was I acting like one? In 10 years could I look back and be proud of what I was accomplishing? No. Why is drinking so normal? Not just one drink, but drunkenness; pure stupidity getting blacked out drunk and wasted? It is literally its own culture that often invites significant conversation: "What will we drink tonight? Let's get wasted. I was so hung over all day. Let's have more shots!" and so forth. Then drinking to the point of not remembering the night as if that is something to be proud of and boast about. That is not accomplishment. That is failure. The type of failure that does not get you closer to success, but pushes you further and further away. Eventually, I slowly began to come to my senses more and more each day. I knew I wanted to stop, but I had no real motivation. When your friends or the guy you are dating drink just as much, it is easy to just continue the pattern. It was not until I was forced to go get a biometric screening at the doctor for work that I woke up.

During a biometric screening, you are required to get your blood drawn and they check everything: blood pressure, cholesterol, blood sugar, etc. In my mind, I knew I was fine. I was exercising on occasion and ate healthy most of the time, so I thought. During my follow up visit, of course the doctor always asks, "Do you drink alcohol? If so, how often?" I always lied and said socially, about one glass a week. Total lie! Socially for me was more like everyday and multiple drinks. I even carried a flask in the car and sometimes my purse, but I did not think of or consider myself as an alcoholic. Many of us do not. Well, the results were in! To break it down for you: A pre-diabetes diagnosis is an A1c (glucose blood sugar) between 5.7-6.4%. My results were at 5.9%, right in the center; I was pre-diabetic. When the doctor informed me, I was shocked. Like how can this be? I am healthy! I exercise and have a pretty healthy diet most of the time. Then I asked her, "Can alcohol lead to your blood sugar levels rising?" "Of course," she said, "alcohol is pretty much straight sugar, especially if you are drinking more than the recommendation." Mind you, according to the Dietary Guidelines for Americans, moderate drinking is up to one drink per day for women and up to two for men. I can tell you now that majority of Americans are abusing their limit. After seeing and listening to my results, I knew I was most certainly abusing my limits. I left the doctor that day knowing I needed to make some serious changes.

The following day I began to analyze everything I was doing including all my behavior. I began thinking what is it that I want in this life. We only are gifted one.

Gifted. Life is a gift and I was abusing mine. I was mistreating the one temple God created and I was doing so through slowly poisoning myself. Not only with the liquid I was willingly pouring into my mouth, but also along with all the toxic waste I was allowing into my mind to influence my thought patterns, actions, and morals that were changing my character for the worse. Family and friends would even mention the change to me with concern. I did not listen. Who were they to tell me? In my mind, I was getting better and having the best time of my life. But I was only falling further behind. Five months earlier my younger brother addressed his concern and though he is younger, he is much wiser. He recommended that I read the book *"The Spontaneous Fulfillment of Desire"* by Deepak Chopra. It was all about meditation and the mind. He would talk about mediation and I would think to myself he was crazy. *What? You are telling me to sit still and in silence for 15-30 minutes of a day and just try not to think?*

That is not possible. I tried it a few times and would always get lost in thoughts. He spoke about what he learned in the book, practicing focusing on your breathing with "so" as you inhale and "hmm" as you exhale. *Weird!* But convincingly enough, I bought the book and I began reading. Then put it down. Just like I did almost every other book. Just like I did almost every other goal. Just like I did almost everything I started including a diet, work, relationship, gym regimen; it did not matter, I would begin and not follow through. Mind you, I purchased the book five months prior to receiving the news that created my shift and motivation to change. It was not until I figured out my WHY for change that I was pushed into action. (*This will be discussed in more detail later in the book.*)

After my doctor appointment, knowing I needed to shift my mindset and paradigm, I picked up the book again. This time I did not put it down. The book goes into mediation on a deeper level and explaining the significance and how helpful of a tool it is to do daily. In this same moment, I was in a toxic relationship with an alcoholic who was in denial. When I told him that I wanted to stop drinking alcohol, begin meditating, journaling and turn off social media, the TV, and begin focusing on fitness and prepping all my meals daily, he thought I was crazy. Why would I want to do that? Exercise regularly? For what? I look fine. Why would I give up drinking, it is so much fun; what is the point of journaling or giving up social media? How will you know what is happening in the world? I knew immediately I could not have him in my life. How was I going to grow being with someone who did not support my desire to better myself? This was in January 2016. I told him beginning February 1st, I was going to make a new commitment and promise to myself. At first, it was only going to be 60 days: February through March. April I would go back home to Tacoma and celebrate my accomplishments with all my friends.

Thankfully, our relationship promptly ended, even before my new journey began. And being single and free from another person's opinions and distractions was the best decision. I declared that I would give up alcohol, social media, any toxic people, not date, be celibate, engage in fitness 6 days a week, develop and maintain healthier eating habits, meditate daily, journal daily avoid TV, and be aware of what I feed myself through my ears and eyes--the music I'd listen to, the conversations I spoke or had, and what I would read consistently for 60 days. It was not an easy process in the beginning, but each day I would remember my **WHY**. Why I made the commitment to myself, as well as the gratification I felt each day I got to cross off the calendar. **(Details of my process and how you can do it too are given in the proceeding chapters). At 60-days I added 30 more, turning my goal into 90-days. It takes 21 days to form a new habit, but 90-days to really break a habit and make a new one stick. 90-days for the brain to fully reset itself and shake off the immediate influence of the old addictions of the past. Hence, I did just that.

So much positivity and growth came from within that period. I gained so much clarity and purpose. My visions became clearer, my mind, body and spirit healthier than ever before. Since then my whole life has been restored and brand new, a new birth. Now, all I want to do is share my journey and *The Blueprint* I created and followed with others. I know the daily habits I practiced and continue to practice will work for anyone, in any area or situation given their present circumstances. These are the daily habits and skills that once possessed will transform your life; and if continued consistently with focused discipline, they will transform your life forever.

Before I dive in let me inform you that sitting down to finally put the ideas in my head on paper has been the most challenging part of this process and journey. It all begins with the thought and idea. Then next is the process of thinking strategically about how to make that dream turn into reality. All of us have dreams, desires, goals, fears and doubts. Many of us have people constantly in the back of our ear, literally telling us that we will fail. Telling you that your dreams are too big. Telling you that you are crazy for even thinking against the status quo. I am here to tell you that you are not crazy at all. You are perfectly sane in your thought process. You're courageous and brave, in fact, for stepping up and declaring to yourself that you will not be of the norm. You will not fit into the box of the world and society's standards. Who is to tell you what to do, other than you? Be weary of outside naysayers and haters. They may even look at you foolishly for investing in this book. They say things like, "I will see you at the end of your journey, right back here with me." I am here to tell you NO! They will not. After reading this book you will have the power to say no to your old ways with conviction and know that you do not want to go back to those old, toxic habits. The newfound feeling of freedom within your mind and the rejuvenation you'll feel within your body will overcome any desire of toxicity from your past. You will look back at the old you and laugh for even being so foolish at one point. You will be thankful you have made the new switch. Have faith and trust me. If you don't, write me a letter explaining why. I can tell you right now, the only reason why you would fail and not succeed is because you did not fully commit. If you literally follow and practice daily what I will teach you in this book, you simply cannot lose. You are, after all, reading this because you have become sick and tired of your current circumstances. Correct? Now, let's change those destructive habits and create new ones that you can sustain! But before we begin, let's first discuss the objective.

Purpose and Objective

The purpose of this book is to help you create a systematic structure and discipline toward success, through follow through and getting in tune with yourself first. While everyone else is sleeping, you are focusing on you; this is your "Me-Time." *Me-Time* is so important, because it is this time where you become one with you and your higher self. Then you can clearly recognize your goals. You will have daily, weekly, monthly and quarterly goals. You will visualize how you need to accomplish each. After that *Me-Time*, it is time for execution, from round 1-12 to 60, to 100 and beyond. This requires a kind of structure and discipline that you will soon possess after reading this book. No matter who you are—a college student, parent, athlete, assistant, laborer, aspiring artist, entrepreneur, professional, doctor, lawyer, teacher—you cannot build anything in your life without structure. Whether it is a business, your family, YOU, your relationship, or anything else that's truly meaningful. You need to create Structural Definitive Habits. You must first create that Solid Foundation. Through this 90-Day Transformational Challenge, which is only the beginning of creating unwavering, consistent habits, you will build the cathedral and empire that you envision for yourself and your life. These first 90-days will help you set the groundwork for the next chapter, to the next chapter and the next. Layer, upon layer, upon layer that will ultimately lead to the creation of what it is you are trying to create for your life. Eventually, you will see each 90-days as a quarter and each quarter you will set to achieve a new goal.

Once you begin, do your best to stay consistent and not waver. There will be challenging days where you will want to give into temptation, but remember your why and your end goal. Choose strength in your moments of weakness and push through the desire to falter. Do your best to stay disciplined and focused at ALL times. You will need to recognize the obstacles you are about to experience in advance. You will need to recognize the people who will try to take away your precious time.

Once you give that person that minute, that hour, that day, it all adds up and it takes away from what you want to achieve. You will need to view time as money; and once spent, you cannot get it back. Therefore, you must spend it wisely. If it does not produce growth or propel you forward, moving you closer to your goals, don't even entertain it. Say no! You need to have the tenacity and ambition to be okay with saying no. Most people are not okay with saying no because they do not want to hurt people's feelings. Successful people become successful because they are willing to do it on their own. They are willing to stand on their own and willing to sacrifice whatever is necessary to obtain and achieve whatever it is they desire to accomplish. Just think of some of the greats or someone you admire.

It is inevitable that you will lose friends and possibly family members. This journey will separate the strong from the weak. Your real friends, the genuine people in your life, will still be there to support you every step of the way. We often tend to be so blinded by the illusion of what our family, friends or society will say or think. I will tell and warn you now at times it can become depressing because as you go through this journey, some of the people you thought were closest to you will not be with you in your darkest hours. But it is in this moment that you must realize: if they were not and are not there during your darkest hours, they were merely illusions, sent here to give your world confusion by creating distractions and holding you back from reaching your true potential. Do not attempt to operate in the chaos created from the outside world. Just eliminate it completely.

Again, this Journey will not be easy. But success is not easy, if it was, don't you think everyone would be successful at fulfilling his or her dreams? It is tough, it is challenging; but these hurdles you will encounter, I assure you that you will be able to jump over. When you do, the road will become easier as you begin to gain greater clarity each day. In this book, you will find *intricate steps* that are tangibly created and packaged for you to practice daily. *The Blueprint*; Let me teach it to you and help guide you to become a better you. The Best You! I can only give you the outline and blueprint to help you completely change your life. But you must fully embrace it, own it and master it. You must take the first step then execute daily.

The key to your future success is taking the necessary preventive action steps now to avoid the potentially detrimental consequences later. Need I say again, having this book in your hand right now shows me that you have already made the first step and commitment to yourself; a healthier holistic wellbeing. I commend you now because most people do not take initiative toward the first step. I am proud of you already! It is crunch time! Let's go!! I guarantee you your life will change for the better. You will see results..

CHAPTER **1**

Rise Earlier - The Daily Routine

"Opportunities Are Like Sunrises. If You Wait Too Long,
You Miss Them." ~Unknown

The morning is the most peaceful time of the day. There is a sense of quietness, joy, and exhilaration knowing that you can hear your own voice. There is no one to disturb you; most of the world is still sleep. It is really the only time of the day that you can dedicate to you. Before all the hustle and bustle of work, kids, a spouse, friends, email, phone calls, traffic etc. You have complete freedom in these first waking hours of solitude. When you begin to rise earlier you will have more time throughout the day; hence you are able to better maximize your time and get more accomplished for whatever it is your heart sets out to do. I rise at 5:00 a.m. each day. Yes, even on the weekends. Might seem crazy, but if you want to achieve massive results, you will need to make massive sacrifice.

27

You will need to reprogram your mind and know each day is an opportunity and you must capitalize and seize every moment.

The first thing I do is wake up, make my bed, rinse my face, brush my teeth, look in the mirror and tell myself, "Today will be amazing!" drink a cold 16 oz. glass of water to boost my energy, and head straight to my meditation corner. I either sit in silence or play peaceful mantras. You can search on iTunes, Pandora, Spotify or YouTube and type in meditation music and a whole list of genres will come up. I always choose the most relaxing ones, usually of nature. I start my timer for 20 minutes and sit in an upright position with my legs crossed, head up, eyes closed, each hand rested on a knee with my thumb and middle finger touching. The fingers in this position represent clarity. There are other finger positions such as wisdom where the pointer finger and thumb touch, but I personally choose clarity because when I begin to center my spirit and come into my intention I wish and desire to gain greater clarity of my wants and desires with each breath. I start the timer and begin to slowly calm my spirit and allow myself to come into the present moment. I begin to give thanks for all that I have in my life. Constantly giving gratitude for where I am in that exact moment and would not change it for the world. I send love to others in my life and others that I may encounter throughout the day. "Thank you, thank you, thank you" I repeat at the end of each sentence. For example, I may say, "Thank you God for blessing me to rise and wake another day, embrace a new gift of life that you did not have to grant me. Thank you for my ability to utilize all my senses; I can breathe, I can see, I can walk, I can smell, I can taste, I can hear, I have shelter, transportation, a job, clothes, food, running water, water to drink, light, and warmth. Thank you, thank you, thank you." Just give thanks for everything and anything for the first five minutes. Then after giving gratitude I ask for peace and love to intoxicate my body through every cell and fiber rushing through my veins.

I then repeat positive phrases to myself: "Love... bliss... knowing... love" with each breath. Inhale and say "love" to yourself, exhale and say "bliss", inhale and say "knowing, exhale and say "love". I repeat this for two minutes. Upon completion of that I declare to myself, "I am beneath no one. I am totally independent of the good and bad opinions of others. I am fearless of any and all challenges." Think, feel, act, be whatever it is that you desire. If you want success think it, feel it, act it, be it. If you want love think it, feel it, act it, be it. If you want to know what the future looks like, build it. I then take another deep breath and say, "Thank you." It is about 10 minutes into my mediation at this point and for the last 10 minutes I begin to focus solely on my breath, beginning to fully embrace the moment and forget about any thoughts of the past two minutes ago, a second ago, and not worry about tomorrow or the next minute from now. I focus on my breath and begin to bring all my intention into my heart. Focusing on the beat of my heart and feeling the love and life flow through my body. I then take this energy and focus on one body part at a time, sending love throughout. I can then begin to feel tingles and the love pulsate through my veins from my heart up to my shoulders, down my arms, to my hands and to the tips of my fingers. Then back up my arms to my elbows, shoulders and down to my belly. Down my thighs to my knees, down to the tips of my toes and back up to my heart. The mind is now empty. I begin to imagine I am near water (this is my chosen peaceful Zen place, you may choose one that best suits you) and I can feel the gentle breeze of the wind tickle my arm and blow my hair. I can feel the warm sun kissing me all over. I am lost in paradise. I feel completely free from the toxicity of the world, away from all distractions in that moment and a sense harmony radiates all around like an oracle of pure holiness. At this moment, the alarm goes off. My 20 minutes are up and it is time to begin the rest of my routine and day (5:30-6:00 a.m.).

I then head to the fridge and grab my pre-made meal one: steel cut oats with blueberries and egg whites with spinach and avocado (breakfast varies, but always consists of protein, healthy fat, whole grains and veggies). I heat them up while continuing to listen to soothing music. I try to stay as present as possible and enjoy every bite. After breakfast, I go and sit in my favorite corner of my couch that overlooks the window and I can usually see the fresh sunshine through the blinds. This is where I write in my journal for 30 minutes to an hour depending on my mood and how much I need to write and express. Within my pre-made schedule I already have an hour dedicated to write (6:00-7:00 a.m.). I always begin my journal with the date, time, day and "Good Morning My Beautiful Queen." I then write about my mediation experience, what I am grateful for, how I feel, any new ideas or epiphanies, things I learned the day before, what I want to accomplish that day. I write about my Top Priorities/Objectives to complete, based off the top three big goals for the next 90-days **(Explained later). I write down growth moments and areas I want to improve and fine-tune. The Journal is a time of reflection, planning, giving more thanks and growth. I then complete my entry and I always end with, "I Love you, Have a Great Day!" Depending on what day it is I will use a positive word that correlates to the letter of the day. For example, have a Marvelous Monday, Terrific Tuesday, Wonderful Wednesday, Tranquil Thursday, Fantabulousenomenal

(Fantastic, Fabulous, Phenomenal all together) Friday, Stupendous Saturday, Superior Sunday and so on.

(7:00 a.m.) I then go and put on my fitness clothes, grab my gear and head to the gym for 60 to 90 minutes. The day of the week determines what muscle group I will be working: Monday- legs & abs; Tuesday- shoulders, triceps & cardio; Wednesday- back, biceps & cardio; Thursday- stairs/cardio & abs; Friday- legs; Saturday- shoulders/back combo; Sunday- rest or yoga. After my workout

(8:00-8:30 a.m.), I come home shower, and dress for work; I have meal two, go through emails and do any follow up for work, pack the rest of my meals to go, then head off to visit clients (10:00-10:30 a.m.) which I have already predetermined at the beginning of the week. All my visits are about 35 minutes to an hour out, so on my drive I always listen to motivational audio books where I can learn and grow in the area or field of my interest. Between visits with clients, I have meal three

(12:30 p.m.) and meal four (3:30 p.m.) which I eat in my car. Upon visiting my clients, I head back home to do more work consisting of checking emails and follow-ups (5:30 p.m.). I am usually finished with work between 6:00-7:00 p.m. and have meal five. At this point it is now self-study time. This is where I do research, read, study and write; working toward whatever top three big goals I have pre-established in the beginning of the quarter. At 9:00 p.m., I have time reserved for cleaning, laundry, small to-do's, and preparation for the next day. I decide and lay out in advance what I will wear for the gym and work, review what clients I will visit, make sure my meals are already prepped and ready to go **(I usually prep for the week Sunday and some-times Wednesday, explained later). At this point it is about 9:30 p.m.; I enjoy meal six (a protein shake) then I reserve the re-mainder time to Face-Time my Honey. We speak for about 10-20 minutes. I then read 10 minutes of a good book, then lights out and sleep at 10:00-10:15 p.m. This was a detailed example of my routine. Yours will be different based on your goals and lifestyle that are unique to you.

Notice that I am not waking up and watching the news. I am not waking up without a mission or a goal in mind. I am not aimlessly going through my day. Everything is pre-thought and preplanned. Nowhere in my schedule is a TV show. Nowhere in my schedule is an outing with friends. Why? Because when you have a vision and a goal and you must constantly be working relentlessly each day toward it. Yes, occasionally you may need to adjust and yes sometimes I plan events with friends. But I always make sure my priorities for the day have been completed. It is fine to sometimes tweak the schedule a little, but always get back on track. You must be stingy with your time, where you spend it and who you allow to enter your space. No one is going to give you your dreams. Dreams take hard, smart work, dedication, and constant sacrifice.

Rising earlier is a way to greet the day with appreciation, knowing that it is a gift and you are fortunate to even have risen, and be alive and well. You can see, hear, breathe, walk, smell, feel; you have all your senses. You have life, your heart beats and your mind is the clearest at this point. Start it out with peaceful thoughts and be fully present. Many of us tend to hit the snooze button until the last minute, then jump out of bed in a frantic rush to prepare for the day. Possibly skip breakfast and run out of time to pack lunch or really enjoy the morning. Maybe you have kids to prepare for school and because you are late, now they are late and rushing as well. Then you are in traffic, racing dangerously down the highway, potentially with precious cargo in the back seat. Rising later begins your day off in stress with your heart rate higher than it needs to be. Skipping breakfast can lead you to make poor choices and grab fast food to satisfy your hunger, which will only lead you to become lethargic and in return, more stressed. This rippling effect usually continues throughout the rest of your day. Why live life always in a rush rather than allowing enough time to enjoy each moment that you have breath? Why not have a solid routine that allows your heart rate to stay at a healthy, constant rate, versus consistently racing higher than necessary?

The mornings bring quietude. There aren't kids yelling, babies aren't crying, and there is less noise from traffic outside. The most peaceful, pleasant time of the day that you can choose to fully enjoy all to yourself, if you allow yourself enough time. The time when you can fully think without distractions, can read, write, meditate, plan, prepare and just breathe. You can witness the sunrise, which in my opinion is one of the most peaceful and invigorating feelings. As if God rose, one of the greatest feats of nature. Changing the room from a midnight blue to a warm, sun-kissed orange. Feeling the sun shine through the blinds as it hits my face, saying, "Good Morning, Hello." Looking out the window with love and assurance that today will truly be an extraordinary day.

Mornings are the time when you can jump-start and kick your energy into full gear. Fueling your body with the proper nutrients to help propel you through the day. This means that by rising earlier you can make sure you are feeding your body a complete breakfast, the most important meal of the day. Without a proper breakfast your energy will run low, your body will go into starvation mode, lowering your metabolism and then potentially storing what you eat at lunch as fat. Most people tend to make poorer choices when feeling starved at lunch. Therefore, I recommend you begin meal prepping (discussed later in the book) to avoid those unhealthy temptations when your options are limited. When you allow enough time for breakfast you can fully enjoy each bite, versus scarfing it down or eating while driving to work. You can sit in your comfortable place, possibly read or listen to a good audio book, and truly enjoy this peaceful time to yourself.

My favorite part about early mornings is the gym. In my opinion it is the most optimum time to schedule for exercise. You can always go in the evening, but I personally find as the day progresses unpredictable events can take place, leading you to miss your evening session. But if you make fitness a priority first thing in the morning prior to any other commitments, you will succeed every time. It is the most invigorating feeling knowing that you put your health first and completed your exercise for the day. Plus, it always leaves you feeling happier and more energized; the perfect combination to give you the momentum to continue that level of energy all day long.

Any successful individual will tell you that they have a morning routine or ritual. It is truly the most productive time of the day. As mentioned, there are virtually no distractions. You will have time to review and set your goals for the day and week, possibly getting a few goals done immediately. You can get extra work done that you may not have completed the day before and so much more. You will begin to get more accomplished during the morning than the average person gets done in their whole day. **(Details of my process and how you can do it too are given in the proceeding chapters)*. These chapters will dive a little deeper into each of my habits practiced and performed throughout each day. Why they are important, their benefits, and how to incorporate them into your life over the next 90-days and beyond. These life transformational habits, if practiced on a consistent daily basis, will improve your overall holistic health guaranteed. These adjustments have made and continue to make an immense positive transformation in my life. Producing greater vitality, happiness, peace, self-esteem, clarity, improved health, stamina, love, wealth, less worry, more goals accomplished and overall greater success since I began my journey. Stay patient, determined and focused throughout your journey and eventually these habits will become a part of you too.

ACTION PLAN & REFLECTION:

1. Write out your current schedule. What are your priorities that you have been putting off? (Reference the chart below)

TIME	ACTIVITY	PRIORTY LEVEL
5:00 a.m.		
6:00 a.m.		
7:00 a.m.		
8:00 a.m.		
9:00 a.m.		
10:00 a.m.		
11:00 a.m.		
12:00 p.m.		
1:00 p.m.		
2:00 p.m.		
3:00 p.m.		
4:00 p.m.		
5:00 p.m.		

6:00 p.m.		
700 p.m.		
8:00 p.m.		
9:00 p.m.		
10:00 p.m.		
11:00 p.m.		
12:00 a.m.		
1:00 a.m.		
2:00 a.m.		
3:00 a.m.		
4:00 a.m.		
5:00 a.m.		

Go through and analyze the areas that need fine-tuning and rate each by importance on a scale of 1-4. 1 is a major priority and 4 you can do without for now.

Urgent Priority.	Important, but not urgent.
DO FIRST	DO SECOND
1	2
Urgent, but not important.	Not Urgent or Important.
DO THIRD	Can do without
3	4

3. Make adjustments, especially to the areas you rated with a 4.

4. Now recreate a new schedule according to top urgent priorities.

5. Start setting your alarm thirty minutes to an hour earlier, and place your alarm somewhere in the room that forces you to get up out of bed. Now you are unable to hit the snooze button. This is so that you begin gradually, but if you are truly ready to jump start into the new you, go all in and set your alarm even earlier: i.e., 5:00-5:30 a.m. Since you'll be rising earlier, I encourage you to also head to bed earlier. Your goal is 7-8 hours of sleep (further details later in the book).

REMEMBER:

**When you are rising earlier, make sure to take full advantage of your extra time. You can engage in the following: meditation or prayer, journaling, breakfast, exercise, goal setting/result producing actions, read, packing lunch for the kids, your spouse, and yourself.

Embrace, enjoy and love the New Morning Routine.
This is the first step to becoming the best version of you!

-Routine Template available for download at www.theelleross.com-

CHAPTER **2**

Mindfulness Meditation

"No Matter How Hard the Past.
You Can Always Begin Again." ~Buddha

Meditation is one of the first musts in my daily routine. It helps center my spirit, align and focus my intention and help me envision what I have preset for my day. It calms my mind and brings a sense of peace deep within. It slows down my breathing and frees my mind from unwanted thoughts. It is the kick-starter and boost to my day; a vital priority and necessity. What is it and why is it so important to begin implementing it into your daily life? Where do you begin? Let me explain.

➢   What it is Meditation?

WHAT: Meditation is a time to come into your center. You can choose to listen to peaceful meditative mantras, or some form of soothing music, preferably without words. Or you can choose to sit in total silence. In this moment, you shall begin to focus on your breath. A deep, concentrated focus, breathing in and out. Then you begin to give gratitude for all that you have, not focusing on anything for which you don't have gratitude. As mentioned prior, I give thanks for shelter, transportation, job, family, health, the ability to have all my limbs and sensory functions, the birds, trees, running water, the gift of a new day and so on.

Why?

WHY: In this moment, you can gain clarity and begin your day with gratitude. Start off the day with a positive mindset. It is challenging to be in a bad mood or think negative thoughts at the same time you are focusing on positivity. In addition to easing the mind, meditation also eases the body. It brings about more clarity and awareness of what ails the body. The deep breathing encourages fresh oxygen flow to the muscles that need it most. Helping soothe and relax the mind and tension throughout the body.

The Power of Coming into your Intention and Gaining Clarity & Focus:

"Intention is a force in nature; it is what creates our reality and orchestrates the fulfillment of our dreams. It is about fulfillment and has infinite organizing power. In order to come into our intention, you must clearly visualize what outcome you want for your day. This could be anything. Increased mental capacity, energy, vitality, enthusiasm for life, and a sense of connection with the creative power of the universe, joy, and love. It could be for material abundance, affluence, success, and higher guidance or creative expression. Then once decided you must nurture this intended outcome in your heart. Let it incubate in meditation, allowing you to be inspired to make choices that will allow you to step out of helplessness and into a state of inner strength and power. Today let us break the illusion of dependency through the power of intention. After choosing your intended outcome, put your intention in your heart and listen with your soul. In those first moments of meditation you must ask yourself, "What do I want?" Do not seek the answers, just ask the questions. Ask and you shall receive. Live with this question. Move with this question, "What do I want?" Soon you will move into the answers. The answers will come in the forms of relationships, situations, events, circumstances, insights and imagination."

–Deepak Chopra: Soul of Healing Affirmations
"Intention" *(An affirmation I listen to daily)*

➢ **What are the Benefits?**

BENEFITS: Meditation is essential because it has so many amazing benefits to your overall health! One of the most important benefits is that it physically and mentally reduces stress. And as a society we know how stressful the day can become with all the endless distractions we encounter throughout our day. Many of us think way too much and our mind goes a million miles a minute, never taking a moment to just focus on our breath, breathe and relax. When we allow the mind to relax and become less distracted on all the nonsense that is happening in the world and in our day, we can enter a state of peace. With meditation practice, the stress-related chemicals like cortisol will decrease and our body will begin to produce chemicals such as serotonin; thus, enhancing our mood. When our mood is enhanced our health and immune system is strengthened and improved as well. Our blood pressure and cholesterol levels decrease. You will age slower which means less gray hairs and wrinkles. It can alleviate headaches and migraines. In return, when you do take the time to sleep at night you will rest more soundly and deeply. During and after meditation your overall emotional stability will improve immensely and any tension, anxiety or depression will begin to subside. Positive thoughts will enter and win over the negative. You will gain greater clarity and focus as to what it is you truly desire. You will be an overall happier person and thus your light will shine onto others naturally! You still may be wondering where and how to begin. Well no worries let me explain my process. You do not need to follow mine precisely. Each of us is our own unique individual, so figure out what works for you and stick to it.

> ## INTERESTING FACT
>
> Meditation has also been shown to improve the ability to pay attention and make decisions. Researchers have analyzed brain scans of Buddhist monks meditating; they found that parts of the brain that help people concentrate and make decisions became more active. The burst of activity was very strong in young monks learning to meditate. Hence, this can eventually be you!

➤ **Where to begin?**

To begin you can choose a comfortable location to sit in silence or play peaceful meditative mantras. Again, they can be found on iTunes, Spotify, Pandora, YouTube or whatever sources you use. I personally use Spotify. Start a timer for how long you plan to meditate and then begin with the most common form of meditation, which is to focus all your attention on the breath. Fully engage within yourself and put all your attention on your breathing to help empty the mind. Visualize a peaceful, white light that illuminates you from the inside out. Breathing in the light and love and breathing out the stress, darkness and negativity. When it begins to wander, just bring your attention back to your breath. As your mind settles and your body becomes more relaxed you then begin to do a scan of the body, starting to focus attention on your physical sensations beginning from the crown of your head and slowly moving your attention downward to your feet, covering every part of your body. As you reach the floor, change directions and slowly move back to your crown. The whole time be fully present in the moment, not thinking about yesterday or tomorrow, not worrying about a minute before or ahead. Be fully engaged moment to moment. Next begin to focus on your current state of mind and mood, how you are truly feeling. Depending on that feeling, think about the trigger to lead you to that emotion. Find out the root and the cause. Observe that emotion, and if it is negative work to release it to the Universe and override it with love and compassion. Allow this feeling to grow and expand and send that energy outwards toward loved ones and others around you. Begin to then focus on forgiveness toward yourself and others. Maybe there was something that recently occurred that you have been beating yourself up about or maybe someone deceived you or caused you harm. Feel that emotion attached to the event, breathe in and say to yourself, "I forgive." Then let it go. After that, dive deep into what inspires you the most right now and why. If you do not feel any inspiration, also find out why. Think of your core values, what moves you and gives you warm tingles inside and makes you passionate. What makes you unique and what you stand for. Think about your most important goals in the moment, for the day, week, month, and year and beyond. How will you tackle each one? Do they make you feel enthralled? Are they burdensome and challenging or will they be simple and accomplished with ease? Rather than feel worrisome of all that you need to accomplish, remind yourself that through time all your desires will come into fruition and the only task necessary is to take each goal one step at a time. Get excited and start to focus your attention on how happy you will be once your big goals are achieved. Think about how happy you are now and how good this emotional state feels. Think about how to make sure that emotion will last throughout the day and increase in your life. Then, continue to stay in this happy frame of mind. Continue your breathing. Eventually the timer will ring and you will slowly begin to come out of your peaceful meditative state feeling a sense of calmness and rejuvenation. The mind will feel free. Your **mindset** is key to how you will move and feel through your day. This daily mental exercise is extremely vital to your emotional well-being. As we should exercise the body, which we will discuss later, we must also exercise the mind. This is where all creation and life begins. Protect, nourish, and care for it the same way you would a new-born baby. Constantly giving the baby love and affection, monitoring, caring, teaching and striving to give him or her the best attention possible to ensure the baby grows to be smart, strong, wise, happy, and healthy.

ACTION PLAN & REFLECTION:

WAKE READY & EXCITED:

➤ Give gratitude and be thankful for where you are today. Forget about yesterday and do not worry about tomorrow. Be grateful for what you have; do not think about what you don't. Know that someone always has it worse. Be at peace and have the abundance mentality.

➤ Now, pick a peaceful and comfortable location in your home to sit and meditate. You can choose to invest in a mat to sit on comfortably, or you can begin sitting on the couch in an upright position with feet 90 degrees planted firmly on the ground. You may also choose to lay flat on your back in a Shavasana yoga pose. Where and however you choose, make sure you will be comfortable.

➤ Establish a playlist of meditative mantras or relaxing music without words.

➤ Set a time frame and an alarm each day reminding you to meditate. Then once you begin, set a timer for 10 minutes. Begin small and then allow your time to gradually increase.

➢ Let your ego go and enjoy this time getting in tune with your higher self.

Key Take Away: REMEMBER:

Take time for you in the morning, relax the mind and mediate.

CHAPTER 3

Your Personal Bible: The Journal

"Go Confidentially in The Direction of Your Dreams.
Live the Life You Have Imagined."
—Henry David Thoreau

What to Journal About? Why it is Important? What are the Benefits?

I consider journaling to be the most important part of the day. Meditation is important, but not over journaling. Cognitively in the brain, we are more likely to hold ourselves accountable or remember to do a task when it is written on paper. Even better, when it is written on paper we can visually see it everyday as a constant reminder. Why is this? Because writing down your thoughts forces you to clarify what it is that you truly want. A journal is *your internal compass and road map.* You can express and convey to yourself your goals, dreams, desires, experiences, ambitions, new skills or other things you have learned, feelings, emotions, gratitude, what you do not want, what you want to eliminate and what you want to add more of, heart breaks, new love, new adventures; really anything the heart desires. When you take the time to do this everyday you will begin to witness growth and change within yourself. You will go back to a month ago and be able to visually see your progress, or where you may have fallen behind and need to pick back up. You can go back and remind yourself of your true intentions and passions. It is you writing down your life story; and a beautiful one it is.

In the morning, depending on how deep my meditation is and how much brainstorming I need to accomplish, I will journal for 30 minutes to an hour. I recommend 15-30 minutes. Similar to meditation, I always begin with gratitude. For the first one or two paragraphs write about everything you are grateful for in your life. "Dear God, Universe, Creator, thank you for waking me up this morning and allowing me to enjoy the gift of life. Thank you for my ability to breathe your air, feel the warmth of the sun kiss my skin. Thank you for food, water, shelter. I pray for those who may lack what I have and I pray to achieve the abundance to be able to give back to those less fortunate. . . Thank you, thank you, thank you." This is a simple example; usually I am much more elaborate and I give my thanks for what I am personally thankful for, and you would do the same. As mentioned previously, when you feel gratitude first thing in the morning it is difficult to feel unhappy or negative emotions. As humans, we are unable to feel happy and sad at the same time. If you are thinking happy thoughts, speaking words of encouragement and wisdom to yourself, your body will follow, and feel that happiness that you are experiencing within, outward. To assist you, I have included a journal with this book. Within the journal, you will write what you are grateful for, how you are feeling, your thoughts, your top three priorities for the day, your goals and inspirations, what you must accomplish that day and more. Toward the end there is a section that reads "free flow from the heart." I am sure when you get there you will keep writing because once you start and your creative juices are flowing, the pen will continue to flow naturally. I always write the time and date at the beginning and sign and write the time at the end. You can structure yours however you would like; the journal included helps guide you with prompts. More details on why and how this will help move you forward toward making your dreams a reality will be discussed in later chapters.

Toward the end of my daily entry, I always write down what it is that I WILL accomplish throughout the day. For example, Monday is leg day (we will get to fitness later), so toward the end of my entry I will write something like. "Okay, that was my entry for today, today I am going to complete XY & Z. I am so proud of you and the woman you are developing into daily, stay focused, stay committed and do not get discouraged, today is going to be a Marvelous Monday! Now go and conquer those legs!" That last note gets me pumped and excited to hit the gym and go all out and upon closing my journal I do just that. I DE-

CLARE and make the decision; I act on that commitment, complete my mission, and then feel amazing after doing so. A journal gets your day started and helps motivate you to take action. You will be articulating what your intentions are on paper. Any time you may feel off, it is great to go back to your journal and review some of your most important entries. I personally highlight and put sticker markers on key entries. By doing so on a regular basis, it helps prompt you to stay focused on your mission.

Naturally as you write and brainstorm, you will figure out what it is that excites you most. What really causes you to feel enraged with a deep, burning passion and desire? What ignites your insides full of ferocious flames? A passion that, when you see others not doing it or doing it incorrectly and you know that you can help them do it better, if you could, and they let you, you would gladly assist! For example, you are a passionate sales person and you see a fellow mate consistently having trouble closing a deal, and seeing them fail makes you frustrated and you want to help. Or for me, it is others not fully valuing their temple, whether that is in fitness or with their mindset. When I see people spend constant hours in front of the toxic tube, who also complain that they do not have a job, or want a better job. What goes through my mind is that they are not being productive; they are not spending their time wisely. Rather than complaining and sitting on the couch, they should be on the computer or in the library doing research to get them employed or figure out what it is they truly want out of life. What sparks you? What drives you crazy? What do you want to change about yourself that will, in turn, help benefit others? Because at the end of the day, that is what it's all about. Helping others by being a better You. Figuring this out will help lead to your ultimate goal!

ACTION PLAN & REFLECTION:

1. Take a moment to **visualize** what it is you truly want and desire. Literally sit in silence, close your eyes and envision your biggest dream and ultimate goal as if you are already living that life right now.

2. Take a standard sheet of paper. Fold it in half hamburger style, then again, and again. A total of three times. Now fold it hotdog style three times. Now open that sheet of paper. You should now have a total of 64 squares on each side, a total 128 squares. Example Illustration Below:

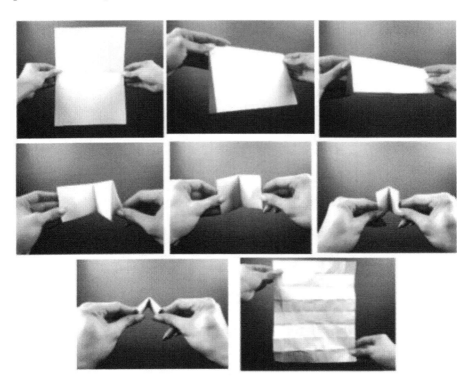

Now take a few minutes to write down descriptive words that naturally come to your mind without thought, words that correspond to your core values, beliefs and elicit the flame within you. That passion and deep desire. Anything that comes to you. Write non-stop until you fill every box. There are no right or wrong words. After all, you will be the only one viewing this list unless you wish to share it with another person. Now go back and review the boxes. What words did you write? Do you notice any patterns? I am sure many of the words are similar. As you take note of these similarities you will notice where your true passion lies. Now it is time to refocus your energy and work toward it.

3. Now take some of the key words and turn them into an affirmative statement of what you want and will work towards each day depending on your goal. For example, words on my list were Health, Fitness, Vitality, Wisdom, Strength, Power, Impact, Communication, Inspire, Learn, Change, Grow, Focus, Success, Self Motivation, Love, Leadership, etc. My affirming statement which I review daily is: *I want to communicate my passion with love and energy, to empower and motivate others to make improvements within themselves to live and lead healthier, holistic, happier lives; through SELF transformational habits.* Some space is provided below:

_____

_____

_____

_____

_____

_____

_____

4. Start journaling if you have not done so already, using the one provided or your own.

Once you figure out what exactly it is that you want, write it down somewhere you can visually see throughout the day: morning, afternoon and night. You can even set a little reminder on your phone to go off periodically throughout the day. I wrote mine down and put it on my fridge. Maybe you put it near your bed, bathroom mirror, or in the car. Just make sure it is available consistently during your day.

Next, make some time during the next couple of days or weeks to:

CREATE A VISION BOARD

People have various theories on vision boards. I have heard negative comments, but the truth is visually seeing what you dream and desire daily sticks in your mind. When you protect your vision, and keep it at the forefront of your mind, it is easier to follow through and naturally make better decisions and choices throughout the day. After all, a vision is only a vision and does not come into fruition until you begin to take action toward making it a reality. Here is an example of mine:

I began my vision board in 2008. At the time, it was simple with only a few items, and over time I added more. There was a time where it was rolled up in the closet and I never looked at it. When I started my journey to a better me I took it out and put it on my bathroom wall where I can see it everyday. I have added along the way. It is awesome to look at and know that some of the items on my board have already come into fruition.

The vision board will help you see your desires daily and you will want to take action. You can create an actual board and make it into a crafty art project with pictures and words that inspire you, or you can write confirming, positive notes throughout the house and on the mirrors so you are constantly reminding yourself of your visions, goals, dreams, and desires. I personally have phrases and words written on the top of all my mirrors, the fridge, and even notes in my car. For example, in my bathroom mirror I have written, "Decide based on Standards, Not Emotions! & Kill Procrastination!" (Shout out and Thank You to Peter Voogd for inspiring the first statement, it truly changed how I was viewing my world at the beginning of my journey).

REMEMBER:

Visualization written on paper, then reviewed daily: morning, afternoon, and night.

Now, take a break. Write your list of items you need to purchase from the store and choose a day this week to get crafty.

CHAPTER **4**

Goal Get It Done. My Journey

"A Goal is a Dream With a Deadline." —Napoleon Hill

Before I arrived to where I am today, it was first only a thought and an idea that resonated within me over and over and over again on a daily basis. I would think the thought and move on to the next, but it always came back to the forefront. I knew that if I wanted to be a holistic wellness and fitness coach and mentor I needed to make personal changes within myself first before preaching to others. I could not be a hypocrite and speak about the negative effects of alcohol if I was drinking, promote regular exercise, eating healthier, making smarter choices, take a social media fast, limit television, meditate, pray, and be positive if I were not taking my own advice. I could not speak about taking huge risks, such as leaving your hometown, family, friends, job, and security to venture off into the unknown without a job or personal connections, if I had not done so myself.

As mentioned, my journey began in Tacoma, Washington. I had my eyes set on becoming an actress and model originally, based on what other people told me I should pursue. But that did not align with my inner drive and passions. Within me I wanted to lead. I wanted to be a business owner, fitness instructor and help inspire and impact others holistically, mind, body, and spirit. But I doubted myself and instead convinced myself that acting and modeling was my passion. If you were to ask me why, my answer would not be very convincing. I could barely convince myself and was mostly just going through the motions. I began to take classes and I worked each day on my craft to become an actress and model. I worked out six days a week to lose weight, not to be healthy, but to be stick skinny. Why? Because I was told I was too fat. Although standing at 5'9 weighing 135 lbs. is small, it is not industry small. I needed to be 115 lbs. To conform to industry standards, I would not eat enough calories, basically starve myself and work out for two hours twice a day. Sometimes I would only eat an apple and crackers. I stopped going out so I could only work and workout. I originally planned to go Los Angeles, California, so I went briefly and did not enjoy it. In addition, I had no family there. My aunt in Atlanta, Georgia, recommended moving there, as it was growing rapidly; so that was my new direction. My journey began in March of 2014 and the set date for my move was October 10th. I had it circled and highlighted on the calendar. I did all the necessary research, planned the trip in detail down to how many miles of travel, the cost of gas, food, hotels, where I would stop and rest, and what day I would arrive months in advance. I worked relentlessly each day toward that date. When that day came, I was ready. I packed what could fit in my car and took off with my mom. I arrived in Atlanta, no job, no friends, no direction, and alone. This is where I made my mistake. I had the vision of arriving, but did not have a vision for after my arrival. The next year and a half a ton of backsliding occurred. Weight gain, over indulgence, alcohol abuse, party addiction, and joblessness; using credit cards for everything and getting increasingly in debt, doubting myself, and facing depression. I began to lose sight of who I was, my core morals and values and conformed to what I was seeing other people do on social media and around me. Feeling a need to fit in when I knew deep down that was not my true mission and purpose. I was rock bottom; thoughts of suicide began to fill my mind. I felt hopeless, worthless, and I wanted to give up. I was unhappy with myself, the choices that I had made and was making. I slept and did not leave my room for four days. My mom recommended that I come home; I knew I could not do that. People were expecting me to fail. People thought the move to Atlanta was the most stupid idea, telling me I have a degree, why not work a corporate job with benefits? NO! I refuse to work for someone else. I want autonomy. How will I achieve that and turn my dreams into reality?

The first step to take you closer to what you really want is setting specific, measurable goals with target deadlines.

"If you aim at nothing, you will hit it every time" –Zig Ziglar

Let's start by talking about the significance of goals. If you don't currently have any, you are doing yourself a grave disservice. If you are unsure where to begin, don't worry. Make sure to follow the helpful process I will show you at the end of this chapter. So, why goals? Goals are vital because they help propel and move your life forward in a positive, upward direction. It is the road map to your dreams and brings them to life. They will keep you locked in with tunnel vision because you will have a visual of where you are headed. This will help allow you to limit distractions, which we will go over later. When you set specific goals for yourself and change your mindset into, "NO EXCUSES, THIS MUST GET DONE", you will gain so much focus that you will learn to say NO to anything that is not aligned with your ultimate goal. You will stop procrastinating because you know what needs to get done and accomplished without excuse. Remember, nothing happens unless you are willing to put in the work. A lot of work will be required. It all begins with the first step, followed by the next, making small incremental daily progress. Then simultaneously, with each step taken, you will have more motivation and get excited with the process of relentlessly doing whatever it takes (morally and ethically).

Top-level athletes, successful businesspeople and achievers in all fields all set goals. Setting goals gives you long-term vision and short-term motivation. It focuses your acquisition of knowledge and helps you to organize your time and your resources so that you can make the very most of your life. Without goals, your God-given abilities and talents are useless. To begin, think about your dream lifestyle. What kind of life do you want to live? Do you want to be debt free? Do you want to be able to spend more time with your family? Vacation when you want? Do you want to own your home? Early retirement? A healthy and vibrant life? Let's start by taking a moment to write down your dream life. Write everything that it is your heart desires. If it is a higher income level, write an actual number: $45,000, $112,000, $200,000,000 etc. Do not be afraid to write a *seemingly* insane number. Health goals, finances, personal, job, relationship, material, travel, freedom, family, kids, and where you want to live. Be as detailed as possible. If your goal is to lose weight, don't just write "lose weight." Instead, write down I WILL be 135 lbs. by August 8th or I WILL be down to 14% body fat and gain more defined lean muscle by August 8th. If you want to increase your income, write: I WILL reach a six-figure income by May of next year. If you have a dream home, write down the color, how many rooms, whether the floors are carpeted or hardwood, or whether you want a garden. If you are unmarried, but desire to marry, when will you be married? These are all just example ideas, but as mentioned, you can write down whatever you want. There are no rules or limits. Start right now. Take about 30 minutes or however long you need.

When you are finished come back. There is some space provided below:

_____

_____

_____

_____

_____

_____

_____

_____

_____

_____

_____

_____

_____

_____

Finished? How do you feel? Are you thinking to yourself that you are crazy? Well don't. Why? Because everything you wrote down is possible. How? Because it's in your heart. Now you must create a game plan on how to get there and achieve those big, audaciously insane goals of yours. And that is what the next step is. We will now write a list of your top priorities. So take about 5 minutes and do just that. Some simple examples may be to begin exercising three times a week for 30 minutes, start working on that big project, begin research to launch your business, spend more time with the kids (a minimum of 2 hours) in the evening, learn a new language or craft once a week, start saving or investing 10% of every paycheck, limit television time to an hour a day, cook three times a week, eat better by buying more fruits and vegetables and packing them for snacks, only order one drink when you go out and tell your friends to hold you accountable. Whatever your goals may be, write them all down and be SPECIFIC and AFFIRMATIVE. Some space is provided below:

CHAPTER 4

_____

_____

_____

_____

_____

_____

_____

_____

_____

_____

_____

_____

_____

_____

_____

_____

_____

_____

_____

_____

_____

_____

_____

_____

_____

_____

_____

_____

_____

Once finished, go through the list and circle or highlight your top three--the main ones that you know you must get done as of yesterday, but keep putting off. Have you circled your top three? Great! Now forget and eliminate the rest of the list. Yes, eliminate it, and if written on a separate piece of paper, throw it away. Why? Because these will be the Top Three Goals which you will be focusing on the most over the course of the next 90 days. You can choose another three after 90-days, once you finish the first top three. Now that you know what you want and you know your top three it is time to set "**SMARTER**" Goals.

> *"If You Want More. You Must Become More.*
> *You MUST GROW Into Your Goals."*
> *-Jim Rohn*

SMARTER goals, for me, stands for Specific, Meaningful/Measurable, Attainable/Action-Oriented, Realistic, Timely, Exciting/challenging and Recorded (there are other similar versions and meanings for the mnemonic acronym as well).

Specific:

What do you need to achieve in your area of focus? Make sure whatever the goal is that it is in line with your core values and morals, not someone else's. For example, your dream is to be a violinist and play all over the world, but your mother really wants you to become a doctor. So for the last 8 years you have been pursuing that, but you feel a continual emptiness and yearning desire as if you are not living up to your full potential. Well I am here to tell you that you are not, you are currently living your mother's dream and she is wishing to live vicariously through your success. Do not be afraid to begin your pursuit now toward your own dreams. Do not think about the time it may take to get there. The time will pass regardless of whether you are living up to your heart's deepest desires or not. Wouldn't you rather be spending that time doing what it is you love most?

Meaningful/Measurable:

Why is this goal important to you? Think of the WHY. Let the why fuel and spark every cell in your body. Do you wish to play the violin because you want to unite people from all over the world and touch their souls through the sound that resonates from within and vibrates outward through every glide along each string, bringing tears through the one of a kind melodies you create? What are the necessary steps and how will you achieve it? When you know exactly what you want, and your why, you will know exactly what you need to do to get there. For example, if you want to be 135lbs. by August 8th, why is this your goal? Do you want to be more active for your kids? Fit into a dress for a special occasion? You know that you will need to have an intervention with your kitchen cabinets and refrigerator and throw away all the no good, processed junk food. Then, stock up on the good, wholesome, ener-gizing food from the earth and not the laboratories. Rule to remember, if you cannot pronounce the ingredients on the labels, then most likely you should not be ingesting that product. After changing out the cupboards, you will notice that you are no longer snacking on the junk, and now opting for healthier choices. You will begin to notice the changes that take place outside as well as within and know you are making progress. This will keep you wanting to stay on track. By measuring your goals throughout the journey, it enables you to stay focused and allows the opportunity to celebrate reaching each success.

Attainable/Action-Oriented:

You need your goals to be attainable so that you are more willing to act on making them a reality. You may have a big dream that may seem daunting to even think about, but that is only because you are thinking about all the work it will take to get there all at once. Instead of overwhelming yourself with everything you need to get done, focus on small tasks and create small baby goals that will help you progress closer to your ultimate goal. For example, it may be a goal of yours to be the top sales person in your company. You first must think of the necessary steps to make that happen. First, you need to analyze what you are currently doing in your day-to-day strategy and figure out what is not working and what areas you need to change. How are you really spending your time during prospecting? Are you making enough phone calls and following up? Are you doing your research before meeting with your potential clients? Are you asking the right questions? If not, you will need to make adjustments. Or maybe you want to lose 20 pounds. Do not think about all the sacrifices you will need to make and the time it will take to be 20 pounds lighter and healthier. Do not try to jump in without doing research on proper technique or going on a crash diet and start overtraining. Rather, take it one day at a time and do your research, first analyzing your current habits. What are you currently putting in your body? How many cans of soda are you drinking a day? Could you possibly substitute that for water or make your limit one to two per week? Are you making time for at least 30 minutes of activity a day? If not, can you adjust your schedule? Could you go to sleep earlier so you can rise earlier and make time for your health? Whatever the objective, you must start small and then work your way up to incorporate more small changes. Next thing you know in a few months you are living a whole new, healthier, lifestyle! When you start small, you will be making incremental improvements each day, getting closer to your overall goal. In one month, you will have made a great deal of progress.

Realistic:

How do you know that you can achieve this goal? This is very important. Know that all progress takes time. Nothing happens overnight. It takes more like 90-days, and then sometimes another 90-days, and so on. Therefore, the quick fixes, like losing 10 lbs. in 10 days, go for it if you wish, but only if you want a temporary fix. Then gain 20 lbs. immediately after and be more miserable than when you started. You need to make LIFE habitual changes to create lifetime results. Therefore, set realistic goals and deadlines for yourself. Set the target date out a couple months, then work on those three vital priorities relentlessly each day until they are second nature. Then you can begin adding more, and adjust as needed.

Timely:

By when do you need to achieve this goal? Again, you need to be SPECIFIC and AFFIRMATIVE. I will reach X by Y to have Z. It is vital to create a timeline for yourself when working toward achieving your goals. Setting a specific deadline will give you greater momentum and motivation along with a sense of urgency to get the small, daily, necessary tasks accomplished. As mentioned, those small steps add up overtime. For instance, when you had a big exam approaching, a championship game, a future vacation, an audition coming up, a project due for work, the expectation of a new child, planning to purchase your first home, or whatever event or circumstance you were preparing for, you did so in advance. Then when the big day arrived, you were ready. With proper diligence and discipline in creating and sticking to the timeframe you create for yourself, you will certainly achieve your goals.

Exciting/Challenging:

You need the goals that you create for yourself to be exhilarating. When you visualize, the ending overall result should excite you. This joy and love that you feel inside will help get you out of bed each morning, enthusiastic and ready to start on whatever is necessary to get you closer to reaching your dream and making it your reality. It should challenge you in the sense that each day, the work done propels you forward. It makes you better and it pushes you to do activities outside of your comfort zone. It forces you to take risks and think outside of the box, or possibly pushes you to learn a new task or skill that gives you a greater advantage in your market. For example, writing this book has not been an easy task. It has taken patience and forces me to dive deep within myself. It's a personal risk to share my story to you, wondering whether I will reach you and help transform your life from the inside out, or inspire you to make positive life changes and begin to develop into your best self. My practice of rising each day at 5:00 a.m. to start my routine and getting to the gym at 7:00 a.m. was not easy in the beginning. It was a challenge, but it was also exciting to know each day I woke with a purpose and a mission to accomplish. Once completed, it is the most rewarding feeling; knowing that I put myself, and most importantly, my health first. As time has progressed I got more of my book completed, and my holistic wellbeing flourished. I could feel and see the changes taking place. Witnessing the progression continued to keep me moving forward, and continues to do so each day. This is what you want for yourself. You want the fire inside you to shine bright each day you wake. You want your goals to challenge and push you to grow and reach your full, limitless potential. Do not set barriers for yourself. If you work toward your goals each day, you have the power to create, change and become whatever your heart desires.

Recorded:

You need to record your goals by writing them down. It is important to write them down since this allows you to make them more tangible. When you write them down, you have taken the first step to making a commitment to yourself and affirming that this is what you desire. Place them somewhere you can review them everyday. You can review and write down your goals in your daily journal, on your daily routine, monthly calendar, or set a reoccurring alarm reminder in your phone. Also, with your calendar you can set small key target dates for mini tasks and mark your deadline for your overall goal. With your goals recorded, you are also able to go back and review your progress, analyze and make adjustments if necessary. Overall, recording your goals will help keep you accountable. I review my goals daily and set reminders for myself throughout the day for what tasks I must get done. I also write them in my journal each day and have them listed on my calendar. It is amazing to go back and see how far I have come, and it gets me excited for the journey ahead. When you begin to implement these habits into your life, you will feel accomplished and motivated to continue to progress further.

ACTION PLAN & REFLECTION:

Now, you will do a similar activity, but this time you will imagine where you want to be in five years? Be as specific and as detailed as possible. Some examples to think about: Home: how many rooms, color, pool, driveway, fixtures, etc. Car: what kind, color, etc. Are you married with kids? What is your career? Where do you live? What is your daily routine? Now grab some paper, your journal or use the space provided below and write; may need additional space. There is no time limit.

CHAPTER 4

The next step is to begin to work backwards from there, breaking down each year into segments and quarters. Year 5: Quarter 1, 2, 3, and 4. Year 4: Quarter 1, 2, 3, and 4. . . and so on. For example – In year 5 I will be... I will have accomplished... In the first quarter, I will have successfully...etc.

Space provided below, but may need additional space:

_____

_____

_____

_____

_____

_____

_____

_____

_____

_____

CHAPTER 4

_____

_____

_____

_____

_____

_____

_____

_____

_____

_____

_____

_____

_____

_____

_____

_____

_____

_____

_____

_____

_____

_____

_____

_____

_____

_____

_____

_____

_____

_____

_____

Now rewrite your current Top Three Goals for the next 90-days:

1.

_____

2.

_____

3.

_____

WHY are these Top Three Goals important to you? Take the time to write down, in specific detail, why each of those goals is important and vital to your future self. For each one, create a powerful statement that you can memorize and post somewhere within your vision that you can see on a constant, daily basis. For example, if your goal is to lose 15 lbs., your statement could be, "I am loving my body and my new healthier, fit self!" Every time you say that statement you will be visualizing yourself at your goal weight. Anytime you get an urge to make a poor health choice, say your statement. It will remind you of your why and your commitment to yourself. Naturally, you will then choose to make the smarter choice. Use the space below to write down your why and powerful statement for each goal:

1.

_____

2.

_____

3.

_____

Now write down the three actions you will put in your schedule to help you achieve those Top Three Goals:

1.

_____

2.

_____

3.

_____

Next, go and share your goals with a close friend or family member to help keep you accountable with your actions steps. Tell them to please call you at the end of each week to discuss your progress. This will help motivate you even more, since you will now be required to give your weekly progress report to someone who can help keep you accountable. You can also keep track of this in your journal. It always feels amazing to look back and see your accomplishments thus far throughout your journey. It can serve to increase motivation to continue and keep moving forward toward greater results.

"Progress is the Ultimate Motivation." -Elle Ross

Finally, remember to plan your week every Sunday or Monday (if that is when you start your week). But choose a specific day.

Then each night before bed review your day (a chapter later in the book). Go through and check if you have accomplished all the goals you had set out for yourself. If you did not, why and what happened to prevent you from achieving your goal(s)? Then commit to adjusting and fixing where it is necessary. Then preplan the following day ahead. Already have predetermined in your mind how the following day will play out. Identify your top 3 priorities then break each down into smaller action steps necessary to accomplish them daily. Each day you should already have set in stone what MUST be accomplished. NO EXCUSES. Visualize prior to falling asleep. Get yourself pumped up to take on the day ahead! Then rise in the morning ready to conquer the day. Decide, then act. Remember to make choices throughout the day based on the standards you have set for yourself, not based on how you are feeling. Make sure you set your standards high and enjoy the journey!

CHAPTER 5

Make Fitness a Priority

"The best project you'll ever work on is YOU." –Unknown

Today, more people talk about their goals and desires to make healthier choices regarding diet and exercise versus taking consistent action towards making it a reality. Remember that excuses are useless and will never get you closer to your goals. Excuses will continue to prolong the process and if you do not take control of your life now, you can most certainly see yourself in the same exact place this time next year and five years from now (if not worse). Starting an exercise routine does not have to be complicated. You can start with as little as 10 minutes a day. Wake up and stretch, then do 10 crunches and 5 pushups. Choose to park your car a bit further when you go run errands or use the stairs versus the elevator. There are so many small, daily changes you can make to become more active. And with food, skip the donut and the Mocha Frappuccino and switch to an apple and Americano instead. That alone could realistically save you 500 unnecessary calories, not to mention all the processed sugar you do not need. Beginning to incorporate exercise changes you drastically for the better. Why would you not want to become better? Physical activity can improve your health, boost your mood, and reduce the risk of developing several diseases that are becoming more and more prominent in today's world like type II diabetes, cancer, and cardiovascular disease. Physical activity and exercise can have immediate and long-term health benefits. Most importantly, regular activity can improve the overall quality of your life.

Regular exercise aside from a healthy diet is key to the success of your overall health. You do not need to go crazy or over the top, by any means. I personally exercise at least six days a week because it helps get the blood flowing and boosts my energy and mood the entire day. Why would I not want to feel that natural high that the body produces when you get your heart pumping and positive endorphins rush through your veins? It truly is better than any drug and can certainly become a healthy obsession that improves your holistic health.

THE HOW & BENEFITS

One of the great benefits of exercise is it helps control your weight through the ability to burn calories. Even if you just exercised for 10-15 minutes a day, consistently over time, you will see a difference. You do not need a gym membership either; there are plenty of fitness videos for free online and most television networks like Comcast and AT&T U-verse offer free fitness channels and videos on demand (at the end of the book there is a website link where you can go to my site and get a customized exercise plan that matches your goals and needs.) So, there really is no excuse. As mentioned earlier, you can park further, choose to take the stairs, do outside yard work or house chores, and purposely leave the remote further away so that you are forced to walk over and change the channel. Really anything that will get you up and moving. This extra movement throughout your day will help combat health conditions and the likelihood of you getting heart disease, diabetes, high blood pressure, cancer, depression, arthritis, stroke, and obesity.

DO NOT WAIT UNTIL IT IS TOO LATE!!

If you choose to sit and do nothing and do not begin taking the necessary steps toward a healthier you now, your doctor will most certainly force you to later. At that point, you will have no choice but to make the switch and it will be a much longer process. Start now, today, and prevent the inevitable.

When you begin, you will start to recognize how awesome the body is and that it can do so many amazing things. With the incorporation of exercise into your routine, all your functions will be enhanced. Physical exercise helps to strengthen the bones and muscles and provides better support to the body as we age. It is also known to improve life longevity. Unlike exercising, there are very few other lifestyle choices that have more of an impact on your longevity. Integrating high to vigorous exercise for an hour a day in your schedule can help reduce your risk of premature death. In addition, physical activity delivers oxygen and nutrients to many tissues within your cardiovascular system that helps them function properly. With exercise, your heart and lungs will function more efficiently. When you exercise, the blood starts pumping and adrenaline levels increase, enhancing your mood and decreasing stress, leading you to feel happier, more energetic, boosting your confidence and improving your self-esteem. Exercise also releases endorphins that are great for managing anxiety and depression (which is why exercise is often prescribed for people suffering from anxiety and depression). It also helps improve your memory, and increases the release of dopamine which helps fight addiction, helps with relaxation, and enhances your creativity.

You will also have a better night's rest and experience deeper sleep, helping you to wake more rested and refreshed. A bonus with incorporating meditation in your day too! And who does not love or enjoy being intimate with their spouse? With regular exercise, since you will have more energy and be feeling and looking better, your libido will increase and so will your sex life. Boom! Bonus! With regular exercise, women's arousal levels are enhanced and men are less likely to have erectile dysfunction. It is a win-win for all parties. But, overall and most importantly, exercise can be fun! There are so many ways to incorporate it into your life, through planning and engaging in individual or family activities, sports, community sports, outdoor activities such as hiking, swimming, taking a dance class or Zumba, or trying something new. The possibilities are endless and there are always new group activities springing up everywhere. Whatever it is, you can make it custom to your liking, enjoyment, and schedule.

"The BODY Achieves what the MIND Believes" -Unknown

Lastly, let's quickly review the importance of proper nutrition. The numbers today regarding most people's health is absolutely alarming. There are more people in debt due to medical bills than any other expense or debt; living a healthier lifestyle can prevent these medical bills. To achieve optimum health, you must incorporate physical activity with a well-balanced diet. We are what we eat. If you feed yourself harmful toxic chemicals through processed foods, fast fatty foods, and sugary snacks with a long shelf life, your body will store most of it because it cannot use it for energy. Ever eat a fatty fried food meal and immediately feel sluggish, bloated, and feel like you have low energy? I am sure you have. It is not a pleasant feeling. Those types of toxic foods will slow you down, cause fatigue, illness, and many other health problems over a long period of time. Those foods can be eaten but in extreme moderation. The rule of thumb to follow is 85/15 or 90/10. 85% of your diet should be healthy and then occasionally splurge the other 15%. Save

that burger and donut for the 15%.

ACTION PLAN & REFLECTION:

1. Go to my website link to download and print your custom calendar for the next 90 days.

www.theelleross.com/shop. ** You will print 3 blank calendar templates.

2. On your calendar, begin to dedicate a minimum of 30 minutes three times a week (preferably an hour a day if possible) to you and your fitness. Find your best time; mine is in the morning but yours may be in the evening depending on your schedule.

3. If you need help figuring out how to get started and a workout routine go to www.theelleross.com/work-outs. There you will find various exercise routines, including a 90-day *B-FIT: Ignite Your Thirst for Fitness* guide. Enter code "IGNITE" and receive the guide for free!

REMEMBER:

-You should always dedicate an hour a day to YOU (even if it is not specifically for fitness).

-With adding exercise into your schedule, you will have prolonged ENERGY throughout the day.

-Look Better, Think Better, Act Better, Feel Better, Be Better

-When you exercise, you are less likely to eat poorly and you will make better and clearer decisions.

CHAPTER **6**

Meal Prep – Spend Less

"You are what you eat." –Unknown

Meal planning is the most effective way to help you stay on track toward reaching your health and fitness goals. It may take a couple of hours in the morning or evening one or two days a week, but it saves you tons of time and money throughout the remainder of the week. It is more efficient and takes the thinking out of trying to figure out what you will eat since it is already packaged, portioned, organized, and ready to go. Have you ever been at work or driving and all you can think about is what you'll have for lunch? Or have mini cravings and the only snacks available are chips, cookies, donuts, and sugary, chemical-filled bars? You think oh, I will just have one. But then you have one everyday that week. It adds up quickly on your waist-line, and leaves you to feel groggy and tired, and possibly even hungrier an hour later. Why? Because you just fed yourself emp-ty calories that did absolutely nothing for your body and those simple carbs will not sustain you over the course of your work-day. When it comes to breakfast or lunch do you always order out? On your way to work you pick up your favorite coffee which is about $4.49 with a bagel sandwich $5.29 and you al-ways tip. Let's just round up to $10-$12 spent every morning on your way to work. Then for lunch someone is sent out to get lunch or order in and you pitch in. The team loves Chipotle, so let's say you spend about another $10-$12 on lunch (a meal and beverage). That is $50-$60 a week, $200-$240 a month and $2,400-$2,880 over the course of the year. Not to mention what you possibly spend in the evening if you and your coworkers head to happy hour for an evening cocktail and even more on a Friday or Saturday night. Do you see where I am going with this? Without preparation, you are destined to fail and slip into poor habits. These habits will lead you to feel less energetic, depressed, and will not only affect you, but others around you as well. You must realize that your body is a temple and you only get one. You must honor, value and take care of the most important person and vessel that supports you each day: your body. What you eat affects everything else and all the other vitals in your body. If your eating is off, your mind, body, and spirit will also be off. So why not start now and prepare your weeks in advance with healthier choices and great savings in your pocket?

Another great benefit to meal prepping is you will know exactly what is going into your body. By prepping your own meals there will be no hidden ingredients, processed chemicals or extra hormones. I recommend wholesome foods from the earth. If you may not always feel up to the task, there are many great meal prep services available that may not save you as much money, but can save you time. Now let's dive into how to get it done.

I personally recommend Sunday and Wednesday. Sunday is a day when, after relaxing, you can hit the grocery store, get the items you need and start cooking. I sometimes prep meals for three days at a time to prevent food from going bad. Then I prep again in the middle of the week (Wednesday), for the next three days. Occasionally, I will prep Sunday for Monday through Friday based on personal quarterly objectives as well as what is on the menu. Depending on what your personal goals are, it is important to know what works best for you. I personally prep five meals out of my day, breakfast, post gym, mid-day meal, lunch, and then dinner, and space them out every two to three hours. My sixth meal is a protein casein shake that I enjoy 60 to 90 minutes before bed. But you may only package your lunches since you enjoy breakfast with the kids in the morning and enjoy cooking dinner for the family in the evening. Your personal goals will be much different than mine, and you may not need to prep as many meals, or eat six times a day. But, I do recommend packing at least two small, healthy snacks if you only pack lunch; and to make sure you enjoy a well-balanced breakfast before work to fuel your day.

Next order of business is to make sure to stick with the staple items. Protein such as lean cuts of chicken, turkey, lean steak, egg whites, and wild-caught white fish. This will be different if you are vegetarian or vegan. Complex carbohydrates such as steel cut oats, brown rice, quinoa, couscous, Ezekiel bread, or whole grain tortillas. Healthy fats such as almonds, walnuts, pecans, pumpkin seeds, pistachios, almond butter, coconut oil, extra virgin olive oil, and avocados. You can enjoy fruit too, such as blackberries and blueberries, but you should generally eat these in the morning with breakfast. Once you know what you need to prepare and what staples you will pair together, create a list and stick to it. General rule of thumb, stick to the outside of the grocery store where you will find the bulk of the fresh ingredients. The middle aisles are always filled with junk food and items you do not need in your cupboard. Finally, make sure to invest in some great food storage containers (like Tupperware), and a food scale, which you can either purchase in the store or order online. Lastly, now that you have everything you need, you will decide portion control of each item based on your caloric and protein goal for the day (there is a guide to calculate that shortly at the end of this chapter). Now you are all set: cook, package, order, store, and then enjoy.

Eat a Healthy, Well-Balanced Breakfast

Starting your morning with a well-balanced breakfast will help get your metabolism going and give you enough energy to sustain you through your morning activities. When you already have breakfast prepped in advance it will cut down the time in the morning and you can already have it prepared to heat up once you get to the office. If you decide to exercise in the morning (highly recommended), then it is great to have breakfast ready to enjoy an hour before or after your workout. In the morning, you will need to start off with complex carbs and protein. Those two items get your metabolism revved up and help energize you for the day ahead. Some simple options are egg whites with whole-wheat toast and almond butter, a protein smoothie, steel cut oats with fresh berries, or a great whole grain cereal and almond milk (you will be able to access detailed breakfast options using the link at the end of the chapter).

A couple of hours after breakfast, it is good to then enjoy a small snack like a veggie such as carrots, an apple with almond butter or a yogurt, preferably Greek since it is higher in protein. There are various options to choose from. This will help catch that afternoon craving before it even begins. Then about an hour later it is time for lunch. Lunch should always consist of a lean protein, veggies, and a complex carb. For example, Chicken, broccoli and brown rice. While this is a simple example, again more details are explained toward the back of the book. Before the workday is over, you will enjoy a second snack like some nuts (such as almonds) or a yummy berry smoothie with protein. And since you meal prepped, these items are already pre-packed and ready to go. Finally, when you get home you will enjoy dinner, readily packed in the fridge and all that is left to do is reheating. If you get a late-night craving after dinner, choose wisely and do not eat anything heavy 2-3 hours prior to sleep. Unless you exercise on a regular basis and are enjoying a protein casein shake right before bed which helps fuel, rebuild and recover your muscles while you sleep. When I say choose wisely, I mean instead of grabbing a Snickers candy bar, enjoy three Hershey's kisses instead. Make SMARTER Choices. Now you may think, "Awe, I can finally relax and enjoy the rest of my evening." NOT!! Now it is time for you to get to that big audacious goal you have been dreaming about all day long. You must optimize your time and maximize each minute you have throughout your day to get you closer to your end goal. If you take a break and decide just to watch Netflix, that time is not being spent wisely. Plus, the whole purpose of meal prep, besides making healthier choices, is to cut your time and money spent down during the week so that you can invest that time and money into the areas that will produce greater results in the long run such as

Your Big Grand Vision. Use this extra time to go back over the goals you wrote down in Chapter 4, along with the action steps to get them accomplished.

ACTION PLAN & REFLECTION:

1. Go through your cupboards and begin to empty out, and throw away/donate any unnecessary items that you know will hinder your progression.

2. While grocery shopping, stick to the outside of the store where all the fresh, wholesome foods are located. Only visit the inner aisles for essentials such as items used for baking, cooking, frozen goods and some whole grains.

3. On the calendar you should have already printed out (if you haven't make sure to do so), plan what day(s) you will meal prep. If you do not already have a calendar and daily routine template handy, you can print out one I have created for you at: www.theelleross.com/shop

4. Go order your Tupperware and food scale if you have not done so already. (Amazon has some amazing deals!).

5. Go to my website to receive my *Nutrtion-Wealthy* meal guide. This guide includes a list of various foods that are beneficial to your health, explanations of why these foods are beneficial, macro and caloric breakdowns and examples of combination foods to use for

different meals throughout the day. It also includes an example 30-day meal schedule that you can switch up or cycle back through over the next 90-days. You will also have the option to get a customized meal plan. In addition, there is a food guide reference at the end of the book. (There is a vegan meal guide option & reference guide available on my site).

www.theelleross.com/meal-plans

6. Begin to fall in love with meal prep. Allow it to become a priority in your weekly routine.

**You may wonder why I choose to eat every two to three hours. The reason why I recommend spacing out your meals throughout the day is because it helps control your hunger and regulate the body's blood sugar, which is critical to either maintaining or losing weight. But rather than focus on losing weight on the scale, focus more on total body fat percentage lost and muscle gained. Muscle weighs more than fat, so remember the scale may not fluctuate, but your clothes will fit better. Best of all you will look better and feel great! And know, meal prep will help to get you there.

How to calculate your Basil Metabolic Rate (BMR):

- **BMR:** The minimum energy required to maintain the body's life function at rest; usually expressed in calories per hour per square meter of the body surface.

To calculate and figure out your caloric goal for the day use the Harris-Benedict equations below:

Calculating Caloric Expenditure		
MALE	metric:	$DCE = ALF \times ((13.75 \times WKG) + (5 \times HC) - (6.76 \times age) + 66)$
	imperial:	$DCE = ALF \times ((6.25 \times WP) + (12.7 \times HI) - (6.76 \times age) + 66)$
FEMALE	metric:	$DCE = ALF \times ((9.56 \times WKG) + (1.85 \times HC) - (4.68 \times age) + 655)$
	imperial:	$DCE = ALF \times ((4.35 \times WP) + (4.7 \times HI) - (4.68 \times age) + 655)$
WHERE		

ALF = Activity level factor	**AND ALF HAS THE FOLLOWING VALUES:**	
DCE = Daily caloric expenditure	Sedentary:	ALF = 1.2
HC = Height in centimeters	Lightly active:	ALF = 1.375
HI = Height in inches	Moderately active:	ALF = 1.55
WKG = Weight in kilograms	Very active:	ALF = 1.725
WP = Weight in pounds	Extremely active:	ALF = 1.9

Equation 1.1: ISSA Complete Fitness Guide Edition 9.0 (Hatfield, Frederick 2016)

CHAPTER **7**

The Night Before

"Prepare, reflect, read, rest." —Elle Ross

The night before is where your tomorrow really begins. How you end your day is equally, if not more, important than how you begin your morning. In life, it is all about the preparation. After all, as the phrase goes: proper planning prevents poor performance. Hence if you set yourself up for success the night before, you will wake up more proactive and efficient. Whatever the task is, set it up in advance. The end of the day should be a time to reflect on your day and prepare for the day ahead. It is important to understand that success starts and ends with your own holistic health: mind, body, and spirit. This is pertinent to your overall energy and productivity. Where you will fall on the scale, either high or low, is significantly dependent upon getting enough sleep. Many people think that they need to work, work, and work, keep working until 3:00 to 4:00 a.m. in the morning, try and function on 3 to 4 hours of minimal sleep, then rise and drown themselves in coffee and poisonous energy drinks. I was once a culprit of this, so I know the struggle. It is not until you take action and responsibility for what is truly important to you and begin to prioritize your life that you will create lasting change and results. You must see your current circumstances and lifestyle as dangerous and detrimental to your future self. The desire for change comes from within and must be more prominent than the desire to stay the same.

Sleep is extremely vital. It is a time for the brain to rejuvenate, the body to heal and repair itself from all the strenuous activity you put it through that day. Many of us believe that our bodies will be able to properly function on 4 to 5 hours of rest. Yes, you will function, but not to your full capacity. It is important that the body get a minimum of at least 7 to 8 hours. Out of any action that we can take to help heal the body holistically and keep it strong and healthy, sleep is the most important. Sleep is more important than food or exercise. The body can go longer without food than it can without sleep. With adequate sleep your immune system, muscle recovery and mood will be better. It helps with weight loss, muscle growth and the maintenance of your energy throughout the day.

Sleep is also important for your brain's overall health. Sleep deprivation can cause cognitive dysfunction, depression, hallucinations, and memory problems. The immune system is weakened, making you more susceptible to getting a cold or flu. It also affects fitness, in that the body needs adequate rest to heal properly to help restore, grow and strengthen the muscles. Without it, the body will be more accident prone and more likely to gain weight. You are also prone to various health risks such as chronic heart problems like heart disease, stroke and high blood pressure. When you continually deprive yourself of sleep your judgment is impaired and you are more likely to eat poorly and often will walk and drive sleep drunk. Studies have proven this to be equivalent to and sometimes even more dangerous than driving under the influence of drugs or alcohol. Simply put, you NEED Sleep. Make it a priority.

Before you shut your eyes and clock in for lights out it is important to prep for the following day. Preparing yourself to be ready, well rested, and energized to tackle the goals you have already set in stone to accomplish. It is great to have breakfast determined the night before (thank you, meal prep), as well as what you will wear, when you will wake, and what you will do as soon as you rise. Regardless of when you choose to exercise, I highly recommend you have your fitness clothes and shoes ready and in sight, set out or in a gym bag. Waking and seeing your fitness gear ready will help motivate you to lace up and conquer your workout, either first thing in the morning or after work. Since you meal prepped earlier in the week, lunch will be ready on the go. Set out the lunch box and utensils on the counter the night before so you won't forget them. Aside from prepping for the next day it is important to review how your day went overall.

Go back through the day's rolodex in your mind and think about areas where you may be able to improve and adjust for tomorrow. Adjust accordingly and fine tune. What tasks could you eliminate and what areas do you need to give more time, energy, and focus? For example, are you spending too much time watching the news first thing in the morning and watching toxic TV before bed, when instead you could be reading a good book, doing lunges throughout the house or researching new leads for your business? Remember, time is money. Sometimes I will even journal in the evening just so I am able to reflect on my day and encourage myself about what needs to get done tomorrow and have it in writing. I also congratulate myself on the accomplishments and progress I made that day. I give gratitude for each experience I encountered throughout the day, good and bad. I thank the bad occurrences for keeping me alert and allowing me to grow stronger through the struggle. I remind myself to let it go and not hold on to the negative thoughts and to refocus my mind on being present in the moment; alive and well.

Another important habit to include in your evening routine is to turn off ALL electronic devices by 10:00 p.m. This means no late-night TV shows, silence your cell phone, no more social media browsing or conversation, stop all text and emails. Make sure to set your alarm in stone and wind down early enough to get at least 7 to 8 hours of sleep. Sometimes life happens, and you may only get 6 hours and if that is the case try and take a power nap for 20 minutes in the middle of the day. Naps are extremely beneficial in giving you a midday energy boost and mind refresher. After setting your alarm, allow your mind to begin to wind down and truly relax. No need to add any more stresses; it is already thinking about the tomorrow that has not even arrived yet. Center your thoughts to the present moment, then grab a healthy book and read something positive for 10-15 minutes before you close your eyes. You want your final moments to be the most peaceful and pleasant. This will allow you to enjoy a soothing, meditative-like sleep of bliss and happiness. You will wake renewed, revitalized and refreshed, ready to conquer the new day ahead.

ACTION PLAN & REFLECTION:

- ➤ *Begin to Turn off All electronic devices by 10:00 p.m.*

- ➤ *Reflect on your day and begin to mentally prepare and plan for the next.*

- ➤ *Evaluate areas of improvement and adjust accordingly.*

- ➤ *Make sure you have everything you need to jump-start your morning ready and prepared the night before.*

- ➤ *Read a positive, educational book 10 minutes each night before sleep.*

- ➤ *Give gratitude to each experience you encountered.*

- ➤ *Finally, rest and relax. Make it a goal to get at least 7 to 8 hours of sleep.*

CHAPTER **8**

Start the Day Off Right & Continue Marching Forward... Left, Right, Left...

"Every Morning Starts A New Page In Your Story.
Make It A Great One Today."
—Doe Zantamata

Now that you have created a morning ritual and routine for yourself, make sure to post it somewhere you can see it daily. My schedule is: rise, gratitude, meditation, healthy power breakfast then fitness or vice versa, then shower and begin to dress and prepare for the day ahead. You should already have your agenda for the day set out in advance, from the night before: for example, what sales calls need to be made, which clients you plan to visit and topics you plan to discuss, and what other work necessities need to be accomplished. Lunch and snacks are already prepared and ready to go and you may have already set out or determined what you will wear for the day. Each hour should have a designation of priorities and tasks already assigned. From rise until rest you want to maximize your productivity. This will all occur once you determine your key vitals, which you should have completed in Chapter 4, and focus solely on the necessities. Rid yourself of the toxic wastes and miscellaneous to-dos that have little importance and do not add value to your overall objectives. We will discuss how to eliminate distractions in the next chapter.

Motto to Live by:

Get Up, Dress Up, Show Up and Be Your Best Self.

You should always strive to look your best and be presentable. You never know who you might meet or encounter throughout the day and it is better to be over prepared than under. People will make judgments on your character within the first 90 seconds of meeting you. First, they will address your appearance, your smile, posture/poise, voice and whether you make eye contact. Can you be trusted? Are you friendly? Are you trying to sell them something (other than yourself)? Will they want to continue the conversation and learn more or move on? You want to be appealing to the eye, but not distracting. You want to be tasteful; with elegance portraying confidence but also a bit of spice. While getting dressed, fuel your mind with encouraging music or audio books. Allow the words or melodies to sink in and soothe your body and soul. Put your mind at ease. After getting dressed, look at yourself in the mirror, and compliment yourself with words of affirmation. Dress your best for success no matter where you are going. Then carry yourself with confidence and assurance. You should feel unstoppable and ready to take on the world and any obstacle that enters your path. When you look good, you'll feel good and that confident attitude radiates outward towards others. It is a magnet that will attract others to you and in return help increase your bottom line.

As you enter your car, the bus, the train, ride your bike, or walk, continue to empower yourself and feed yourself good food for the mind. This could be good uplifting music; I personally prefer a great audio book. In my opinion you can never stop learning and there is always room for growth and improvement. When you stop learning, you begin to slowly die from within and wither away. The mind is a powerful instrument that constantly needs to be fed, fueled, loved, and challenged. Strive to make it stronger, wiser, and better than the day before.

Think about it, we as a people spend tons of time in the car. As much time as you spend in your car, especially with added hours from traffic, you can learn and grow so much! The commute is the one time you have to yourself, uninterrupted. It is just you and you have the power to make that time **me-time**, aka, **growth-time**. Do not stress about the drive or traffic. Take this time to pray and be grateful that you even have a car, thankful for the roads to get you to your destination, thankful that you are alive and well. The numbers of deadly accidents that occur on the roads today have skyrocketed to insane rates and are only increasing. Practice peace and patience when you drive. Your life is more important, so please stop the texting and driving. As you are playing your audio books your mind will be focused on learning and distract you from the fact that you are sitting in a parking lot on the freeway and moving no where. Forget about that and get lost in the words of the book.

To figure out where your time is currently going, go back and reference the end of Chapter 1 where you created your top priority schedule and routine.

There are so many wonderful audio books and educational podcasts out there today. With the advancement of technology, it is a shame how many people do not take full advantage of the era that we live in. This book, along with many others available in an audio version, are great tools to expand your mind, knowledge and education. But do not just listen and learn it all, you must make sure to implement what you are learning into your daily life. The chapters you have read thus far have provided you with lessons. Those lessons, with daily practice and incorporation into your routine one at a time, can help transform and improve your life. Then, over time, the new habits that you create will be imbedded within your subconscious and become second nature. That is the whole point of creating these foundational habits, reprogramming your inner self, then applying the concepts and changes you are making on a consistent basis.

After your productive day, now you are either on your way or already home. If you have a family, take time out to be present in the moment with them, fully and actively engaged in the conversation and interaction between you and them. If you are out at dinner with friends, do the same. Do not be glued to your phone the whole time, checking your social media feed. This is not only rude, but also usually pointless. I talk more about the detrimental effects of being glued to your smartphone, and how to break away from social media, in the next chapter. If you are single and at home, don't be sad. Being single is actually pretty awesome. This is the best time to really get to know the true you. Adventure to new places in the city, take on a new hobby, get in tune with your creative side, or learn a new language or subject. Or better yet, begin to brainstorm and create an outline and game plan for how you are going to achieve the goal you have in mind over the course of the next 90-days! That is why you have purchased this book in the first place. So again, seize every opportune moment you have available.

ACTION PLAN & REFLECTION:

- *Remember to Get Up, Dress Up, Show Up and Be Your Best Self each day.*

- *Be fully engaged and present in every encounter you have with others.*

- *Download the Audible App from Amazon: IT IS AWESOME!!*

- *Invest in a couple amazing books in your field of interest, or subscribe to some educational podcasts on your music media app that are aligned with your passions and interests.*

- *Throughout the day, listen and repeat until it is ingrained within and you have begun implementing what you learned into your daily actions and habits.*

- *Remember to always feed your mind good food.*

- *Enjoy!*

CHAPTER **9**

Eliminate ALL Distractions

"Starve Your Distractions. Feed Your Focus.
Eliminate the Unnecessary." –Unknown

When it comes to eliminating distractions know that in order to move to new heights, you will need to make room in your life. Therefore, it is time to clean house, take out the trash, scrub the floors, maybe repaint the walls and purchase some new furniture to make your house (your life) more vibrant, organized, and less cluttered. Distractions can come in multiple forms and take you off course in the blink of an eye. You cannot change them, for they are all around us, but you can destroy them from interfering with your progress and personal development. You may think you are in control, that is, until your mind begins to aimlessly wander to the biggest distraction of all:

your smart phone. When we wake in the morning, the first thing many of us tend to reach for is our phone. Before we even get out of the bed we may check our news feed, so anxious to find out everything we missed while we were asleep. We scroll through the tweets, snaps, Instagram pictures and Facebook newsfeed. Then we may enter the bathroom, phone glued in hand as we sit on the toilet, then on the sink counter while we are brushing our teeth. The phone stays close by while we are getting dressed and even while eating breakfast; while we aimlessly scroll, and look at mostly nonsensical content. We allow our minds to consume nothing but junk as soon as we rise, not even realizing the effect most of that content has on the mind and in return the effect that it has on the start of our day. The elimination of phone content absorption will be the first task on the list of many. It is today's number one distraction and I personally believe is at the top of the list as being probably the worst distraction in most of our lives. Many of us would not even know how to function without one, figuratively speaking.

Hopefully as you have been reading this book, your phone has been away, resting in silence, and you are focusing all your attention on being present in this precise moment as you read the words on the page.

In order to truly reach your full potential and your goals according to your set deadline and target date of achievement, you will need to make great sacrifices. Essentially, anything that does not propel or move you closer to your goals should be rid from your system and schedule now. This will include social functions. Unless it is a special occasion that cannot be missed or a networking event where you know you will meet new prospects that will help generate income and an increased revenue stream, just say "No, thank you." This also means it is time to limit your smart-phone usage. If it is not leading to further productivity, put it down. When you are all in toward making your dream your reality, days of the week no longer matter because each day is a fresh start and brand new beginning. In today's modern society the mass majority dread Mondays, embrace Wednesdays and look forward to 5 p.m. on Fridays. Friday, they attend happy hour somewhere, poison their body with alcohol like there is no tomorrow, get silly drunk to the point they cannot walk or remember the night before and wake the next day with a massive hangover. They can barely function, sleep half the day away, recover and then potentially do the same thing over again on Saturday evening, only to recover again on Sunday. Or better yet, attend a Sunday brunch with bottomless mimosa specials. The weekend is filled with junk food, alcohol and frivolous spending. Only to then wake with the attitude, "Ugh, it is Monday already #SadMiserableFace" and go through the same mundane routine week after week, month after month, year after year. Then ten years pass and you wonder where your life has gone. If only, I wish I would have, I should have, I could have but. . .. Excuses and regrets follow.

Now, imagine if you took hold of your life by the horns, got on for the ride, held on for dear life and did not let go. Where would you be then, and what could you have accomplished? Well guess what? You can. You just need to be courageous enough to believe in yourself and have the *willingness to do* day in and day out relentlessly, not letting anyone or anything stop you. Therefore, you must embrace the most powerful word in the dictionary: NO! Begin today: say no more, and yes less. Limit the toxic tube/social media: minimal to none. The time you have been taking to binge on Netflix, put that off. The time you spend watching your favorite television series, record them for later. Trust me, you are not missing out on anything and that time spent on the couch can now be redirected to more result-producing activities. No social media, unless you are building or currently generating revenue and an income where you can leave your day job. You will survive just fine without it temporarily. Try it for 30 days. If you think that is too much, try one week. If that seems too daunting, start off with one day. Take baby steps toward going all in and being fully committed. When I took the leap and challenge to go without social media, I did not test the waters; I dove right in headfirst. I went 90-days and it was the most liberating and insanely productive quarter of my life. Now, again, if you use it and it is generating income, only post and check messages as necessary to assist you in achieving your financial goals. No meaningless scrolling and browsing. Think about how often you are on it now. Again, the moment you wake and constantly throughout the day, even while on the toilet, brushing your teeth, eating, and dining with friends when you should be present with them. Most of the content on social medial is meaningless, pointless foolishness, and can literally waste hours of your time each day. Social media is consuming our generation and most of the world's life. We have become addicted to caring what others think and needing to feel validated by complete strangers who we will never meet nor know. They will not know who you really are, nor will you them.. Much of it is a hoax and façade. It is truly a temptation. Do not compare yourself to the images you see and instead, become your own, individual standard. Begin to truly fall in love with yourself and stop caring about the opinions of others. Be you.

Hence, when you say no, you do not need to explain why. Just say no and move on.

To begin this journey, go to all your social media accounts and temporarily deactivate them. Unless you are currently using them for work and they are generating revenue, deactivate them right now! Yes, I know for many of you this seems crazy. Like, "What! Are you serious? How am I going to stay in contact with my friends and family?" Your friends and family should have your personal number. And remember, this is only temporary and you will survive.

Not having social media isn't life threaten-ing, so relax. If you have a favorite TV show, put that on pause too. Try to limit or eliminate the time spent in front of the TV for the next 90-days. If you just considered the 90-days and thought, "OMGAWD!! That is such a long time! I do not think I can last that long," stop now and just focus on day one through seven, then two weeks, thirty days and so on. Think about your goals and objectives. How important are they to you? If they are not striking a nerve of urgency, then they probably are not big enough and it is time for you to stop here and go back to the beginning of Chapter 4 to reevaluate the drawing board. You can come back to this point once you are mentally ready.

Question, "Why?" **WHY**: because that time will be spent on a different area of your life that needs some nurturing, such as family time, fitness time, learning something new, working on your passion, and ultimately transforming into your best self. Turning off and deactivating your accounts will help limit that meaningless scrolling you do randomly throughout the day (and waste hours doing it) without even realizing. When you see successful people, do you think that they just arrived to where they are and all their achievements just happened overnight? Of course not. It took sacrifice, dedication, and strategically allocated time. Take a moment to breathe in deeply, close your eyes and envision what you truly want to achieve over the course of these 90 days. Imagine that you are already there at day 89 and reflect on how much you have grown thus far and all you have overcome and accomplished. Do you have a smile on your face? I know that I do. Now realize that in order to feel those exact feelings of euphoria and happiness of getting to your end goal, it is the risks and sacrifices you make that will get you there. Sacrifice is what will set you apart from the crowd.

Next, analyze your circle of influence. Your circle of influence is extremely crucial to reaching your next level of growth and achievement. Your surrounding peers should be aiding instead of hindering your personal development. You are who you surround yourself with. It is said that you are the average sum of your surroundings. For example, if five of your friends all drink heavily, eat poorly, and aren't active, it is only natural that you will be the sixth and slowly pick up on their poor habits. But if you are in the company of the opposite, with a healthier circle of friends who enjoy healthy dining, outdoor activities, and limit their drinking, you will naturally over time be the sixth. Which habits do you want to pick up on? You do not want to be around negative, toxic people who weigh you down. I am sure you can think of a friend right now who only calls you to vent about their problems. You think you are being a great friend by lending an ear to listen, but honestly that friend is detrimental to your mental health. They are presenting and pouring all that negative energy into you. I am sure once the conversation is finished your mood has changed and you may even feel like you need to help your friend and their situation. Well, know that you do not. Their problems are not yours; let other people's issues and dramas be just that, theirs. You have the right to kindly decline their phone call or in a polite manner directly inform them that you are not interested in listening. You have your own obstacles to overcome and do not need to have others intruding and distracting your thoughts.

If you surround yourself with friends who have poor money management skills and spend frivolously, using credit card after credit card to keep up with the Joneses and are always inviting you to go shopping, gladly decline. You do not want to spiral into the debt pit that they are in. Observe and watch others and think: do you want to live that life; would you trade places with them? If the answer is no, adjust your circle.

Your circle should inspire you, motivate you and lift you to new heights. Your circle should challenge you and push you to be better each day. If you are striving and want to make millions or billions you must surround yourself with those people of like minds and visions. You must surround and associate with those who are already making and have what you desire. Many successful people were once in the same place as you and usually are willing to help share their knowledge and expertise with others. Do not be afraid to ask or go out there and network. You will never know unless you try. The worst thing that can happen when you do take that leap of faith is getting a, "No" response. And big deal, "no's" come a dime a dozen, don't give up, keep trying and just move onto the next. Remember that is just one "no" from one person or group, and there are countless others you can connect with. And often you are just one "no" away from the perfect "yes" opportunity or acquaintance. Be patient.

With true friends, you should be able to share your crazy ideas and goals with them without judgment and they will hold you accountable when they see you veering from your path or goals. Those friends are far and few to come by and sometimes you just need one—or, if you are mentally strong enough to redirect and critique yourself, you may find that you are your own best ally and friend. Hold yourself accountable to higher standards and declare to the world your new ambitions. When you declare to others, it gives you the feeling that now you need to go out there and prove it. Not for others, but primarily for yourself, your most important asset. You do not want to look back on your life with regrets. If you are looking back now, stop because in this moment you have the power to change and redirect your path to a better you than you were yesterday. Being conscious that each new day you are progressing and moving forward.

Another harsh concept that you will need to grasp now is that you will lose friends along the way. Not because they do not care about you and vice versa, but because you will now be acting outside the normality of the group. You are growing and most likely they are comfortable where they are and seeing your progress makes them uncomfortable. You now think differently, act differently, move differently and they are not moving on the same frequency or same direction as you at all. They will attempt to bring you back down to their level of understanding and thought. They will taunt you and tell you that you are being too uptight, that you need to live a little or live it up with them. But what is living it up? In society's terms, most define "living it up" as over indulging in unhealthy foods and drinking until you can barely walk and waking the next day hung over. Or possibly a shopping spree, spending your whole first check on one over-priced material item or out at a venue to celebrate "getting paid" with your friends. Where does that get you? Better yet, where is that getting your friends? Observe their growth over time; you will discover that most are in the same place now as they were the year before and the year before that; making no forward progression. Is that what you want for yourself? If your friends or the people in your circle are not adding value to your life and making you better, then limit or eliminate them. Not to say you cannot occasionally say hello if they reach out, but trust me they will not reach out. Some may only reach out if they need something and trust me there is no point in keeping that relationship. Do not bother reaching out to them either, as there is no point in putting energy into others if they are not helping to build or add to your overall objective and goal. Bring value, joy, growth and positivity into your life. Hence, you must be willing to lose those friends who are not accepting of the **New You**.

ACTION PLAN & REFLECTION:

1. Take a moment to analyze your circle of influence. Grab a piece of paper or your journal and write down the first ten people that come to your mind. It is fine if you do not have ten.

1.

_____

2.

_____

3.

_____

4.

_____

5.

_____

6.

_____

7.

_____

8.

_____

9.

_____

10.

_____

2. I assume the names you wrote down represent the people you consider yourself closest to, or those with whom you at least associate regularly. Now evaluate each one, the pros and cons. What character traits do you like most or least? Who can you learn and grow from? Who do you admire? (Reference chart below).

Friend	PROs	CONs
1.		
2.		
3.		

4.		
5.		
6.		
7.		
8.		
9.		
10.		

If they have more cons than pros, most likely they are a distraction and during your growing process it may be best to limit your interactions with them. As you continue to grow, you will learn who the culprits are and the ones that will stick by your side.

Finally, go through and number each person **1, 2 or 3.**

3 – means you will need to cut them out of your life through your process. 2 – means minimal contact to occasional association. 1 – means you should surround yourself with this individual more often since they help uplift, push, and motivate you toward excelling and reaching your dreams.

CHAPTER **10**

Constantly Focusing on You

"Success is not something you pursue. What you pursue will elude you; it can be like trying to chase butterflies. Success is something you attract by the person you become. For things to improve, you have to improve. For things to get better, you have to get better. For things to change, you have to change. If you grow; your money will grow; your relationships, your health, your business and every external effect will mirror that growth in equal correlation."-Jim Rohn

This is probably the most important section and concept to grasp out of all the chapters in this book. It encompasses every other chapter and area we have covered thus far. Each section is giving you the tools to better YOU! Make yourself your greatest asset and ally. At the end of the day, at the end of this journey, you hold the key and the power to make your dream your reality; no one else. You are the one that needs to make sure you wake up each day and set out to conquer and achieve the goals you have set in stone to overcome and accomplish. You are the one that makes the decision of what to feed your soul, mind, body, what you watch, who you surround yourself with, and how you allow others to treat you. Whether or not you exercise, allow time for your body to recover and rest, think positively, give gratitude, spend wisely, work smarter, love yourself and give love to others, practice patience, go to networking events, invest in books, and choose to take action.

You are also the one who allows doubt and fear to seep in. This self-doubt and fear creates distraction, worry, anxiety, depression, and poor nutrition choices. You are the one who will choose to pursue your true passion, or decide to self sabotage and choose to do the exact opposite to distract your mind from getting the important tasks done. You are the one who may allow those poor choices to lead to depression and cause you to be lazy and sit on the couch all day while watching the toxic tube. You choose to associate with others who lack ambition and hold you back or try to convince you not to pursue your biggest dreams and goals. You are the one who allows yourself to think negatively. You are the one who may waste time on social media aimlessly scrolling, seeing what others are doing instead of focusing solely on what you can be doing to work toward the improvement of yourself. All that distraction will cause you to not take advantage of opportunities to network and grow. Rather, it will facilitate your overall decision to continue to make poor choices and in return you'll become your own worst enemy. Which would you rather choose? To be your own best friend and greatest ally or your worst enemy and constantly self-sabotage your holistic health and growth? As one of my favorite mentors stated best, *"What is easy to do, is also easy not to do."* –Jim Rohn.

Think about where you are investing most of your time right now. Some of us put more time into our job than we do ourselves. We will work so hard to help promote and grow someone else's business and dream and neglect our own. I am sure most spend it aimlessly without thinking about their future or the long term, negative effects and consequences of their current daily actions and habits. Any entrepreneur or successful individual will tell you that the best investment you can make is the investment in yourself. Before you invest in anything else you must invest in yourself first, as that is where you will gain the greatest and highest yield on return. When you read books that promote a healthier mind, enjoy food to help fuel and energize your soul, exercise to increase your heart rate and gain better circulation, listen to motivating audio or inspiring soothing music, or watch educational television, naturally your overall wellbeing will be renewed for the better. You will enjoy life more, you will be more motivated, and you will accomplish more, work smarter, and be happier. Trust me, your bottom line will increase substantially. Again, if you desire to have more, you need to become more. You will need to grow into your goals.

You need to always be working on self, consistently and relentlessly each and every day. Create unwavering habits. Forming new habits takes time, but if practiced daily the process becomes easier and easier, then you can fine tune, correct, and become better. There is not a limit to how well-rounded you can become. Even the greats strive to be better. Elon Musk, LeBron James, Stephen Curry, Michael Jordan, Oprah Winfrey, Richard Branson, Darren Hardy, Tony Robbins, Dwayne Johnson, Howard Shultz, Lady Gaga, Beyoncé, Jay-Z; those are just a random few extremely successful individuals who are consistently working on their craft to become better than the day before. They are no different than you and I, the only difference is how they invest and spend their time. We are all given the same 24 hours in a day, but many of us don't create a strategy of how to get from point A (our current circumstances) to Z (our goal and overall objective and vision). Study those who bring you inspiration and for whom you feel admiration. Choose a mentor. What do they do differently? What resonates with you the most? Now how can you incorporate those actions into your daily rituals?

At the end of the day all you have is yourself; hence you should always focus on SELF first:

SELF EMPOWERING LIMITLESS FOCUS.

"Are you learning everyday? Are you growing every day? Are you being challenged everyday? That is the key to success. The day that stops happening the world is going to start turning in the wrong direction for you." -Donny Doitch

ACTION PLAN & REFLECTION:

We went over a routine earlier in the book, but now it is time to get specific.

1. Take a moment to review and reflect on your current daily schedule and where you are allocating most of your time. Are you dedicating enough time to YOU? Or is most of your time going to others?

2. Specifically, create a timeline from the time you wake up to the time you rest your head back on your pillow at the end of the day (go back and review the end of Chapter 1). Do you notice any specific patterns or poor mismanagement of your time and energy that you can redirect to a more productive task?

Example: Spending 3-4 hours in front of the TV watching pointless shows, when within that time frame you could have gone to the gym (possibly watched your show on a cardio machine), studied a new language, read a new book, made something healthy to eat, or worked on a new project that assists in your future business.

If you haven't already, go to www.theelleross.com/shop to print out your sample template to fill in and create your daily schedule.

3. Next, write down the specific tasks or areas that you would like to allocate more time to. Space provided below.

Example: Start work on that project, begin writing that book, register to take that course, read a good book, exercise, cook, spend more time with the kids or spouse, etc.

_____

_____

_____

_____

_____

_____

_____

_____

_____

_____

_____

_____

_____

_____

Now go back to your current schedule and adjust as needed. Work this week to incorporate at least three of the activities that you have wanted to make time for but continue to make excuses to not do or neglect. Then as time progresses, incorporate more of the new higher priority tasks. Eventually, you will have a whole new schedule that is goal-oriented toward productivity and working toward the development of your best self.

This routine should be somewhat like the schedule you created for your top urgent priorities in the first chapter. The objective and reason we did a similar activity is to begin to get this routine in sync and imbedded within your mind and subconscious that eventually your new routine will become second nature; you will create new, daily, healthier habits.

CHAPTER **11**

Go Above & Beyond. Stay Focused & Monitor Progress

"Always Deliver MORE Than Expected." –Larry Page

Much of society will go to work and work hard to impress their boss while he/she is present, will be at church and praise God and portray an outward holiness for others to see, will go visit their parents or friends and put on a façade as if all in life is well and excellent. Then as soon as one is not in the presence of their boss go back to slacking off and browsing social media or not making the necessary phone calls, leave the church and head to happy hour cursing at every car along the way, arriving to meet with friends only to gossip about what so and so wore to church or the weekly reality TV drama, then leave your parents venting about how much they get on your nerves and potentially partake in your toxic drug habit or lifestyle. This type of lifestyle is unhealthy. When you lie to others you are only lying to yourself. As mentioned previously, lying to you is worse than lying to others. It is the most detrimental internally. When you lie to you, you will never grow and you will always hold yourself back from reaching your full potential.

For example, someone who clearly has a drinking problem but continues to convince himself that he is not an alcoholic. Or in front of others does not drink, but as soon as he walks in his door pours himself a glass which leads to a few more. Therefore, you must always, even when no one is looking, put forth your best effort, choose growth in the moment, speak life, and make healthy choices. Not for others to see and give you validation, but for yourself. Your future self will thank you most candidly. Always do your best in every area even when no one is watching. At the gym do a few extra reps, and stop taking random, unnecessary breaks to scroll through your phone. With your clients if you work in sales, always follow through on your promises. After a long day of work choose not to give into toxic social pressures.

It also helps to monitor your progress. For example, if you have decided to give up drinking or another toxic habit, possibly create a calendar where you mark off each day you did not give in. You will be able to see how many days you have accomplished not giving in to your temptation and it will inspire you to continue and not break the streak. In addition, it is great to keep a schedule to assist in holding yourself accountable. This coincides with the calendar. You can either keep a physical schedule or you can keep track with the calendar in your smartphone. I suggest a smartphone specifically because I am sure that it goes wherever you go, and it can vibrate or sound alerts and reminders. There are numerous apps that help assist in scheduling. I personally enjoy using Awesome Cal. It is just that, awesome! I literally list and write down everything! What I spend, where I plan to go, who I will meet, appointments, tasks to accomplish, when I'll go to the gym, what workout or body part I will exercise, what I eat, etc. A popular app for tracking what you eat is MyFitnessPal. In the beginning of my journey I used it all the time. But now my routine has become so ingrained within, habitual, I no longer use the application. Now, throughout the week my eating regimen is consistent. "What I eat may vary, but my meals always include the four important staples: proteins, fats, veggies and complex carbs." I now can eye my food and determine the weight in ounces. Eventually, you will be able to do this as well. Sticking to a routine is great and extremely rewarding. Everything has a place in your day and if you need to adjust you can do so according to top priorities. As the day progresses you will get to cross out or check tasks off. I call it "The Master To Do List." And it will give you such gratitude and excitement to check items off. It is also great being able to look back over your week and visually see how much you have gotten accomplished then look forward with excitement to conquer the week ahead.

When moving through this journey and reviewing your schedule and routine, yes at times it may appear daunting. It should! If your dreams don't scare you, then they are not big enough. If you share your vision with others, there will be some who try and shoot your dreams down. But do not let that discourage you. You must always be thinking about the bigger picture and objective. Know all the small changes that you are making now, compounded over time, will grow into massive changes later, giving you drastic, life-changing results for the better. As long as you remember to consistently choose growth in the moment. Even in the moments where you feel weak, or may want to give up or break down, make sure to take a moment to close your eyes and visualize your future. The one you dream about at night before bed and daydream about throughout the day in traffic or at your workstation. The overall why you have even purchased this book and are reading and actively participating. It is because you know your true potential and you are ready to tap into it and become fully engaged. Don't stop now or revert to your old habits

Don't move backwards. Continue to keep pressing and moving forward toward the new and better, holistic you.

ACTION PLAN & REFLECTION:

1. What are the top five things that distract you most?

1.

_____

2.

_____

3.

_____

4.

_____

5.

_____

2. Write down five areas where you know you slack off.

1.

_____

2.

_____

3.

_____

4.

_____

5.

_____

3. Now write down why you allow those items to distract you and a plan of action of how you will begin to reduce or eliminate that distraction.

1.

_____

_____

_____

2.

_____

_____

_____

3.

_____

_____

_____

4.

_____

_____

_____

5.

_____

_____

_____

4. Now write down why you believe you slack off in these areas

and a strong reason why you know you need to go all out, along with an action plan on how you will keep this promise to your-self.

1.

_____

_____

_____

2.

_____

_____

_____

3.

_____

_____

_____

4.

_____

_____

_____

5.

_____

_____

_____

5. Now sign and date the line below as a promise and commitment to yourself to take action.

Signature: _____

Date: _____

CHAPTER 12

The End is Only the Beginning

"Every New Beginning Comes from
Some Other Beginning's End." – Seneca

This book was written with the intention to help you come out of your shell and spread your wings. The wings that you have kept hidden. The wings that may possibly be damaged or scorned from past experience, pain, or grief. Wounded from the negative comments of those you considered close to you; who may have deceived you. You may have been and still are fearful of the judgment from others, but there is no need. Do be wary of the choices you are making right now or were making before your new journey. You and the choices that you made have determined where you are in this moment. Do not be a zombie and continue to go through the motions without purpose. Without a vision and goals, you are essentially slowly killing yourself within and it trickles to other areas of your life. You may have seen your outer appearance change in a way that dissatisfies you and your mood diminishes. In return your family and relationship life falters as well. Your income is stagnant and you are not prospering; all because you choose to just go through the motions. You choose to give your power to others, who essentially run your life. You have given away control. It is time to take your power back, take a leap of faith and choose to mentally shift and reprogram your mind, body, and spirit from the inside outward.

I hope that thus far, through the activities and writing exercises in this book you have noticed the changes within. I hope that your mood is better and you have greater energy through your morning meditations. That through the practice of morning meditation you are now able to fully come into your intention and visualize how you want your day to pan out. And with each action you make smarter choices to achieve the goals that you have now learned to preset for yourself. Through the action of setting goals, you now have a clear direction of how to achieve your overall objective.

Most importantly, I hope that you have truly figured out your WHY. Your WHY is what will continue to keep you focused and continually progressing forward. Even in the challenging times, your WHY will help push you through. I hope that with your new routine you have strategically predetermined set times that are specifically dedicated to you and your overall wellbeing. I hope that you now incorporate a fitness regimen a minimum of 3 to 4 days a week, if not more. That with the meal prep you are now not only saving money, but you are also helping save your health and trim down your waistline. I hope you are enjoying good, wholesome, and healthy foods. Lastly, I hope that you understand who your most valuable commodity and asset is, **YOU**. You now are putting yourself and overall wellbeing first and above everyone else. I hope that you are now allocating more "me-time" in your day, as well as investing in expanding your knowledge. I hope that you will continue to strive to learn new skills and apply the principles to your daily life. That you realize wherever you choose to invest your time, energy also flows, therefore you must be selfish with where you spend it and with whom. Overall, all the habits and steps learned throughout this book are the foundational building blocks to help you achieve and grow to new heights, far beyond what you have ever imagined. Allowing you to no longer be stagnant, and instead advance into your full potential.

In order to continue to expand and advance into your best self, know that the action steps performed throughout this book must be maintained. Make sure to work hard each day and try your best. Yes, there will be times where you splurge or you are not able to commit fully on certain days due to family or friend engagements, holiday travels and vacations, or unexpected circumstances. It is natural, and life happens. But the key is to immediately get back on track and working toward your mission. Once one goal is achieved a new one should be set in its place. Therefore, you are always working to be better. Never settle, you can always be more tomorrow than you are today. Hence, continued growth and progression is key to reaching your full potential and at the end of each quarter, always have new goals set in advance. Remember, **you should always be focused on the betterment of you, improving at minimum 1% each day.**

We are an evolving and ever growing species. As babies, the world was a foreign land where we had to constantly learn and adapt for survival and we loved it. We embraced new environments with vigor and enthusiasm. Yes, in the beginning we were skeptical and timid, but once we got our feet wet we were all in. Somewhere along our journey we allowed our brightness to dim. And as adults, some of us have hidden that light so deep within that it has made us cold and bitter. I hope through this journey you have stopped hiding in the shadows and come back to the forefront and began to radiate for the world to see once again!

Know that the journey that you have now entered is a lifestyle and not a temporary fix. Greatness is not something you do once in a while; it is something that you should strive for on a regular basis. This change is a resolution that you have decided to make to yourself. Commit and go all in! Any resolution that is made today with intent to conquer, must be made again tomorrow. Know that success is never owned; it is only rented and is due each and every day. Hence you must change your appetite and realize that the disciplines you create now may seem challenging, but you will crave to do them tomorrow and they will become so natural. The sacrifices you will make today and throughout this new journey won't even tempt you tomorrow. Your appetites will change through your willingness to do. This is the power of intentional habits and the overall objective of this book.

"Though no one can go back and make a brand New Start. Anyone can start from Now and make a brand New Ending."
-Elle Ross

TAKE AWAY

To get to the next level, you need to make growth part of your daily agenda. You must do something that increases the value you bring to your business, your work, your clients or customers. It's not very complicated to change your current income level. You simply need to offer more value to the marketplace or your field of expertise. You do that by bettering yourself in everything that you do.

Everything you do, do it with dignity and with purpose. Make it your goal to become irreplaceable and become so great at what you do that others cannot ignore you. If you are consistently investing and building your character, skills and overall value, you will advance further than the majority and it will be economically inevitable that you will find greater opportunities. By consistently learning and expanding your mind, knowledge, and skills, your value increases and you will naturally stand out against your competition. You must continue to study, be unique, and set yourself apart from the rest.

You also want to make sure you continue to set your attitude above the rest. Your personality, character, and values are everything. Those first impressions are crucial when making new acquaintances. Therefore, you always want to think, speak, act, look, and be your best. How you treat others is only a reflection of yourself. Love yourself with a positive, happy attitude and naturally that energy will radiate toward others.

Through learning you will begin to become in tune with your higher self. You will become aware of your weaknesses and strengths, allowing you to determine what areas you need to fine-tune and possibly delegate to a more skilled person. For example, I am not a master in technology. I can choose to learn the craft myself or focus on another area more beneficial to my success that I am already good at but can still fine tune; then hire someone to help build and construct the technical side of my business. But, I may choose to still peek over one's shoulder so I can learn bits and pieces because I am always eager to understand and acquire a new skill. There is never a downside to connecting with others who can lift you up and aid in new developments for your dream or business. You want to surround yourself with those you can learn from while you continue to grow. There are no limits to your success when you commit to growing and becoming more valuable. You are always in control regardless of your circumstances. You always have the power to change and write a new chapter in your book, the story of your life. You are a gift and not a curse. You have just been waiting to be unwrapped.

Overall, the key to reaching your full potential is not stopping after your first 90-day transformation. Stay consistent and continue to strive to reach for new heights, always expanding and enhancing your skills, abilities, and mindset further. Even if you faltered off track for a day or two, do not get down on yourself, just refocus, re-center, and align back toward your vision ahead.

Make sure to not overfill your plate and keep it simple. Sometimes we act as if we are competing in a decathlon, being pulled in multiple directions with many events to complete. You are the fastest at the 100m dash, but you want to run the 400m, do the hurdles, long jump, and high jump. Instead of putting 100% of your effort into the 100m dash, you are giving 5-15% here or there and it is slowing you down. Direct all your energy to one event. To one mission. To one goal at time. Perfect it, master it, and complete it, then focus on the next one. A then B then C, **FOCUS**. Otherwise, nothing will get done and completed to its full ability. Coach Wooden said it best: *"Become Brilliant at the Basics."* Once you master one task, one new habit, then you can add something new to your regimen and plate.

As just mentioned, be sure to always be taking consistent action forward. Without consistency, you will never see your dreams and desires come into fruition. Through your consistent efforts and seeing results, you will gain more energy and confidence, which will also give you greater momentum toward progression. You must always be improving your mindset and emotional in-telligence. Be open-minded, be willing to take risks and step out-side of your comfort zone.

That is where the journey toward real success truly begins. And do not be afraid to fail. Embrace it! Failure is an opportunity for learning, a potent teacher and scheduled stop toward success. It is an important part of a solid foundation upon which success is built on.

FINAL WORDS

True success will begin and start with SELF. Know that you'll need to create a paradigm shift within the mind. Your current way of thinking about your health and body has drifted off course. You have given up on self and due to lack of self-love, and you have unconsciously been abusing your body. You'll need to create new self-awareness and self-love. Create a solid **WHY** for the decision you have made to **START** on a new path to recreating **YOUR BEST SELF**. Make sure to take the time to write it down, then place it somewhere you can see it everyday. That reasoning must be set in stone and so strong that nothing can break it. We only have one body, one Temple, one life. Why misuse and abuse it? **Value YOU**. This is only the beginning and if you don't create a why you will most certainly fail because you will lose sight of the importance of why you are taking action. Why are you preplanning meals? Why are you rising earlier? Why are you changing what you feed your mind and soul? Why are you scheduling you in your day? Why are you getting your body active? Why are you making healthier food choices and decisions in general? Remember and know that temporary and immediate gratification is just that, **temporary**. And the consequences of those choices can be detrimental and long-term. But the disciplines and daily practices you are creating will replace these detrimental habits with ones that won't feel comfortable at first, and will be challenging, outside of your comfort zone and feel unusual at the beginning. Know that those feelings too are only **temporary**, and the positive effects, the new habits created will eventually feel natural and become the new norm and soon take over your old habits. But do be mindful, old habits will want to creep back in. Be strong and don't allow this. These new daily habits you create will have extremely beneficial rewards and impacts on your growth. Positive outcomes. Your mindset will shift. You'll feel more energized, happy, youthful, agile, thrilled, and exhilarated throughout the day.

Your vision for your health will become clearer and a rippling effect will charge through your veins, putting you on a new wave length. And most importantly, you'll begin to see the outward results! But it must start from within. Trust me, you will feel and see the difference. This sense of self won't come over night, but I promise you it will through time, as long as you stay committed and determined to succeed. Visualize your final destination. I believe and have faith in You. But you must believe and have faith in Yourself. Choose to be your best friend instead of your worst enemy. Fall in love with You. And congratulate yourself for making the **VOW** to **SUCCEED**!

Yours in Love & Health,

Elle Ross

The Journey does not end here, now it is time to share your knowledge and growth with others. If this book lit a new spark within, has changed your thought process, improved your mindset, has transformed your life or inspired you in any way, please share the love and message to others. Give the gift of growth and enlightenment to someone else. Share your story and join the community of others committed to bettering themselves as well as others. Together we can make a huge dent in the universe changing and transforming one soul at a time.

To join the movement, stay up to date on upcoming, events, promotions and product launches make sure to subscribe at

www.theelleross.com

As well as join the Facebook Group: FITSPIRATION

And for continuous motivation check out my blog and vlog:

www.theelleross.com/blog

www.theelleross.com/motivationelle

THANK YOU!

IT ALL BEGINS WITH A CHOICE
Power Plate
TIPS FOR TRANSFORMATION

Nutrition-Wealthy © 2017 Elle Ross

WATER

Strive to stay hydrated all day long; drinking water, tea or coffee without sugar. LIMIT juice, milk and dairy. Opt for almond or coconut milk instead. AVOID sugary drinks such as soda and alcohol.

HEALTHY OILS

Opt for oils that are rich in mono-unsaturated and poly-saturated fats such as avocado, extra virgin olive oil and canola oil. AVOID trans and saturated fats like butter.

Healthy Proteins
30%

Vegetables
40%

PROTEINS

Strive to eat white wild or farm raised and lean proteins. Such as fish, chicekn and turkey. You can also eat a variety of beans and nuts. LIMIT red meat and cheese. AVOID bacon and other processed meats. Also when possible remove the skin from meats to help lower cholesterol and fat consumption.

VEGETABLES

Strive to eat a variety of colorful and vibrant veggies. Some excellent options are leafy greens such as spinach, kale, arugula; carrots, broccoli, cauliflower, Brussel sprouts, peas, asparagus and green beans. **Notice, most of the items are GREEN.

Whole Grains
20%

Fruits
10%

FRUITS

It is great to eat a variety of colorful fruits. Some of the top superfruits include blueberries, blackberries, grapefruit, oranges, bananas, apples, kiwi, grapes, strawberries, papaya, avocado and tomato (Yes those both are considered fruit.)

WHOLE GRAINS

Strive to eat a variety of whole grains. Such as steel cut oats, brown rice and quinoa. Look for 100% whole grain on lables and choose whole wheat products in greads and past. AVOID white refined processed grains

49175172R00117

Made in the USA
Columbia, SC
19 January 2019